WITH LANGUAGES
in MIND

WITH LANGUAGES
in MIND

MUSINGS *of a* POLYGLOT

KATÓ LOMB

Translated from the
Hungarian by Ádám Szegi

Edited by Scott Alkire

TESL-EJ Publications
Berkeley, California & Kyoto, Japan

Originally published in Hungary as *Nyelvekről jut eszembe...*
by Gondolat, Budapest, in 1983. Copyright © 1983 Gondolat.

The translator and editor express their gratitude to Dr. Maggie Sokolik
of TESL-EJ for her continued enthusiasm for Dr. Lomb's work, and to
Dr. Lisa Vollendorf and Dr. Swathi Vanniarajan of San José State University
for their recognition and support of this project.

Special thanks to Dr. Reiko Kataoka and Dr. Larissa Chiriaeva of SJSU
for their careful review of the manuscript, and to Hunter Greer
and Mark Handy for their fine copyediting and proofreading.

Thanks also to Dr. Keiko Kimura of San José City College for acknowledging
our efforts to share Dr. Lomb's work with the English-speaking world.

All footnotes are by the translator and editor except where noted.

Library of Congress Cataloging-in-Publication Data
Lomb, Kató, 1909–2003
With languages in mind : musings of a polyglot / Lomb Kató;
translated by Ádám Szegi — 1st English edition.

English edition copyright © 2016 Scott Alkire
Library of Congress Control Number: [forthcoming]
ISBN 978-1-4951-4066-2

I. Szegi, Ádám. II. Title.

Cover: *Seville*, Andre Lhote, 1922

TESL-EJ Publications
Berkeley, California & Kyoto, Japan

10 9 8 7 6 5 4 3 2 1

To the memory of my father

Preface

~

IN COURT, the accused have the right to present their defense in a last appeal. The author of a book can use the preface to mitigate her crime.

"Your Honor! I committed the deed with premeditation and with the knowledge that the author of a book on education for the layman faces no fewer dangers than Odysseus did when sailing from Troy to Ithaca."

If we are renowned in our discipline, we will face the Scylla of contempt from our scholarly colleagues: An expert should write for her peers in academia, not the general public. If we are outside of academia, our way will be blocked by the Charybdis of distrust: "Where is the degree that qualifies you to publish your view?"

I wrote this book because it is mostly academics who have written about languages. These experts presuppose considerable philological knowledge that is generally not typical of interested but non-theoretical readers. Few books have dealt with languages at a popular level. That said,

Popularization involves restrictions and simplifications

I am guilty of this charge. I secretly hope that interest will guide the reader to further study.

The role of the popularizer is a modest one. We don't say anything new, just quote others.

As early as half a century ago, when I was a college student, I didn't understand why no recognition was due to the one who "created a tenth book out of nine."[1] But it has been a long time since Farkas Bolyai[2] alone could represent or develop the knowledge of his age in mathematics, geometry, philology, grammar, music, medicine, and social science. Since then a flood of information has threatened to engulf us. What have we gained from it? It positively demands filtering and summarizing.

My own experience learning languages and answering loads of questions by mail and at authors' talks has proven to me that it is worth reflecting on the relation between man and the proof of his humanity, language.

A nation lives in its language,[3] but even more so does the entirety of nations, humankind. "Language indicates the birth of man," painter Károly Lotz wrote. According to linguist István Terts, "The emergence of language...is identical with becoming human."

Man can speak, and speech is unique to man. To describe his development, anthropologists usually mention *Homo erectus,* the Upright Man, and *Homo faber,* the Toolmaking Man. Early man was born into a world unsuited to his body. To change it and survive in it, he needed words.

Homo sapiens, standing at a higher level of development, wanted more: not only to change the world (prophets and missionaries) but to understand it. Today, scholarly anthropologists are modestly content with getting to know it.

Referring to *Homo loquens* as the Talking Man is redundant.

---

1. Reference to the short story "On My Favorite Textbook" by Ferenc Móra.
2. Hungarian mathematician and polymath (1775–1856) who founded the study of non-Euclidean geometry.
3. A saying usually attributed to the 19th-century politician István Széchenyi, considered "the greatest Hungarian."

Talking Man is a pleonasm, as is "round circle" or "aged old man." All we can really study is *Homo articulans,* the Man with Articulate Speech.

Even animals are capable of non-verbal communication. The flattering slinking of cats, the dream-chasing morning whistle concert by quails, the dance of bees to give work instructions, the teasing and strutting of male peacocks—they are all encoded messages. They don't stand comparison with human speech. They are triggered instinctively by the stimulus of perception, their elements cannot be combined like speech sounds, and there is no reciprocity: the opportunity to reply to messages.

Apes have a remarkably advanced calling and alarm system. Yet no one has ever succeeded in teaching them, even the smartest ones, to speak. An American couple, the Gardners, got the closest with a chimpanzee. The chimp was able to communicate at an elementary level with sign language, using her fingers. But articulated speech is a species-specific feature of humans.

It is a sad contradiction that we don't find the study of language—grammar—a human-friendly, approachable branch of knowledge. This proof of humanity has been painfully dehumanized by making it abstract and abstraction, as we know, is one of the highest intellectual faculties.

Grammar is a boring subject for our students, at most worthy of studying for good grades. For adults, it is a tedious chore. Its symmetry does not delight them; its rules bore them; its irregularities discourage them. Today's techies are definitely averse to it.

Grade school pupils meet the abstract linguistic rules at the wrong age and in the wrong form. Basic grammar concepts are abstractions of simple phenomena that have been second nature to them for years. Three trees, three hills, and three stars must have been concrete reality for our ancestors long before the complex and abstract concept of "trinity" was born in their minds.

We know the case of Molière's Mr. Jourdain, who was surprised to hear he had been speaking in prose for 50 years. Little Susie and Charlie, too, find it difficult to grasp that they select parts of speech, use participles, and construct words with prefixes and suffixes.

The ability to speak is genetically coded into every infant. Yet infants learn to speak according to their own individual development—i.e., ontogeny. Until the age of five or six, we are all independent language learners attending an intensive course. Family, preschool, street, and television compete with each other to teach us how to travel as safely as possible in the intricately designed, sky-high palace of language.

This palace has been under construction by millions for millennia. A never-ending project on such a gigantic scale, where everybody has their say, cannot be perfect. To use another metaphor, man tailored language to his body, but he cut it badly. Language will always be a patched garment. It keeps getting poorer or richer as it tries to accommodate new concepts while at the same time maintain itself in an ordered and rational fashion.

It is this phenomenon that makes it interesting to wander the halls of the palace of language, to which this little book offers itself as a guide.

The magic word that makes the locks of the palace gates spring open by themselves is still unknown to me. Many expect a simple formula along the lines of, "Take a tablespoon of a five percent solution of dichlorine-carbazoimide-tetraphenyl-acetate every night. Shake before using."

Well, there is no such thing. What exists is persistence, diligence, and a genuine interestedness in the language. This last term is often shortened to interest, which can be misleading because interest and interestedness can mean different things.[4]

The light beam of interestedness illuminates a wider slice of the world than interest. That is why I ventured to areas beyond just language learning. The light beam of my interestedness will randomly shine into this and that province.

Without any particular design, I will stitch words into words and interrupt myself often as I report what comes to mind regarding languages.

Interestedness plays a decisive role in language learning

The root of interestedness is the Latin *inter esse:* to be inside, to be between.

Our education system, unfortunately, cannot put the student in the center of linguistic events. Our curricula are exam-centered, grade-centered, and textbook-centered. The student, the subject of education, somehow remains outside the language to be acquired. But László Németh[5] wrote that "personal involvement and the desire to experiment can make all kinds of work a labor of love and a formative power." Only communication that addresses us and concerns us can open a gap in the wall of the "foreign" language to be acquired. (I put "foreign" in quotes because I find it rather displeasing. It may be enough to build a barrier between us and the new language.)

---

4.   In Hungarian, there is no confusion: *érdek* signifies interest as a benefit and *érdeklődés* signifies the state of being interested (from the verb *érdeklődik* "be interested"). However, "interest" in English and other languages can be vague because it can signify both concepts (Italian *interesse*, French *intérêt*, Russian интерес [interes]).

5.   Hungarian dentist, writer, dramatist, and essayist (1901–1975).

Half a century ago, children of "good" families acquired languages in private lessons. Children of the "best" families were raised by Fräuleins, misses, and mademoiselles. The nanny system was very effective because the instructor used the most personal form, the most suitable one for memorizing: the *imperative mood*. It is still referred to by educators as the golden tense.

The usual schedule of private lessons was two classes per week. Even this fairly sparse exposure to language made it possible for the pupil in approximately three years' time to reach the level of active speaking skills and language production.

Today's courses generally cannot achieve this, despite much more developed methods of education. Not only is less time given to an individual, but also this one-to-one relation—this *inter esse* or being in between—is missing.

To better illuminate my message, let me approach the issue from a great pitfall of language learning, vocabulary. It is difficult to remember that "nephew" is племянник [plemyannik] in Russian and *sobrino* in Spanish. But if you memorized these words by linking actual people (Andrew or Steve) to them, the vehicle is born right away, ready to deliver the desired term when needed. We have incorporated the new word into the reality of our lives. The word in the new language doesn't link to the native-language one but rather to the *content* behind it.

1

~

A PERSONAL EXPERIENCE of mine illustrates the truth of learning words through associations. A few years ago we visited the Dobšinská ice cave in Czechoslovakia. We had to wait a long time at the entrance. We were with tourists from Bratislava. They were so perfectly bilingual that perhaps they didn't notice when they spoke Hungarian and when they spoke Slovak. Bored of waiting, I started asking them how they said this and that Hungarian word in Slovak. They hemmed and hawed in reluctance. Torn out of context, the word didn't summon its Slovak equivalent.

In education, memorization of a word usually requires association with a phrase in the mother tongue. Indeed, there is no simpler way of assessment and self-checking than testing how many words on one side of a page you can recall by studying their equivalents on the other side. A bad method! A word is not a pet dog that listens to "Fluffy" or "Buddy" and runs to greet us, yelping readily as soon as his name is uttered.

If we try to recall the foreign-language equivalent of a word by focusing on its mother-tongue counterpart, we are like the pole-vaulter who tries to launch himself over the bar from the base of the stand without a run-up. For recalling a desired term, a run-up is essential.

You can hit your target only by stepping backwards in your thinking. This is a law of mental activity. According to Arthur Koestler, all kinds of thinking presuppose the command to step back to take a better leap forward.[6] The surrounding words (or situation) into which we retreat is the *context*.

I mention this so frequently that I am afraid I will be nicknamed Kati Context. But it is context that leads you and guides you in learning words. If your mind is oriented to French while you are trying to communicate in German, and you come across *Maisonne*, you will first think of some derivative of *maison* (house) instead of "Sun of May." If you are thinking in English and not German and come across *Brotherr*, you will think it is "brother" with a typo rather than bread-giving master.

Which of you hasn't had the experience of your mind going blank when in conversation? A well-known name or phrase you have used hundreds of times is on the tip of your tongue, but you can't say it. You rack your brain in annoyance. Then you give up and just paraphrase the name or term, or fall silent. Much later, when you're not trying to think of it, it suddenly pops up in your memory.

What happens at such times? Racking your brain in annoyance causes a surface tension in your mind which blocks the paths of associations. When the tension dissolves and these paths open up, you can travel deep to where the expression is resting in your subconscious, embedded in its context.

I think everyone who has ever spoken a foreign language has met another, similar phenomenon as well. A well-known, widely used expression won't come to mind in language X because it is pushed out by its equivalent in language Y. For example, let's say I am speaking French and I urgently need *ramoneur*

---

6. Probably a reference to the idea expounded in his book *The Act of Creation*. Koestler was a Hungarian-British author and journalist (1905–1983).

(chimney-sweep). Sometimes all I have is its German equivalent, *Schornsteinfeger*, resounding in my mind's ear.

What takes place at such times in the wonderful switchboard of our nervous system, the brain? Is the line—which is supposed to transmit the information—busy? Is there only one socket for this purpose, and once it is occupied by the plug of a phrase in another language you must resign yourself to paraphrasing it?

It is not only context that helps you recall the phrase you're looking for. I will cite an example from my own experience and another from an account I heard.

I cudgeled my brain for days for the name of the Kremlin clock tower. The word wouldn't come. Then, as I was turning the dial of my radio one day, the familiar song of the chime-clock rang out. The very minute I heard it, the term for this kind of tower sprang to mind: Куранты (Kuranty).[7]

The other story was told to me by a young mother. She had to take an exam in a very difficult subject while pregnant. To prepare for it, she recorded the required material on audiotape. She played the tape over and over while knitting little pants and jackets.

When she took the exam, she was hardly able to answer the questions. She was in danger of failing it until she mentally pictured herself knitting; in her mind she wove stitches with an invisible cotton thread. This recalled the material she had listened to for hours on tape, and she managed to survive the exam with a passing grade of 2. A few weeks later she gave birth to two beautiful little boys. She couldn't help but wonder what would have happened had she gotten the excellent grade of 5. Would she have had quintuplets?

---

7. A generic name for a striking clock with chimes.

Context is your dictionary

Context is the only reliable dictionary. At the beginning of my language-learning career I realized that dictionaries can really only help you if you already have a sense of the word in question and how it is used. After all, a word is not a whole but a fraction. If you treat words as wholes, you will come off like the German who studied Hungarian from a dictionary. When he found a Hungarian pen pal, he fell prey to the double meaning of *lieber* and started each of his letters with "Rather Steve:"[8]

Still, dictionaries are indispensable: They specify, refine, and enrich our existing knowledge. For me, they are exciting and delightful. I confess with Amy Károlyi[9] (Somewhat Frosty Poems): "Window rose / window wing / window eye:[10] / Dictionary / With your beauty / I can't vie."

It is experience in the world that orients you in using a language. This is what gives me hope that interpreting and translating will not be taken over by machines.

Computer science was especially optimistic in the early 1970s. Its representatives were proud to aver that their machines could construct sentences having as many as 1000 words. The momentum later came to a halt; they are hardly closer to the goal now.

Machines to teach spelling, known as "I say it, you spell it," have been with us since 1978. They praise and scold aloud: "Well

---

8. *Lieber* in German means not only "dear" but also "rather, preferably." The Hungarian mistaken phrase is "*Inkább Pischta!*" instead of the correct "*Kedves Pista!*"

9. Hungarian poet and translator (1909–2003; incidentally, the same lifetime as Lomb's).

10. In order to convey the original impression, translations are literal. "Window rose" (*ablakrózsa*) is meant as "rose window," "window wing" (*ablakszárny*)— "casement," and "window eye" (*ablakszem*)—"pane of glass."

done!" or "Wrong! Try again!" In cars, a speaking dashboard can warn the absent-minded driver, "You forgot to fasten your seat belt" or "Your oil level is low." And talking phone books have been proposed by the Bell Telephone Company.

These innovations will certainly succeed in America, the homeland of gadgets. However, I don't think they will replace humans in translation and interpreting for the time being.

As of now, a computer speaks only machine language. If it is addressed in another language, it shakes its head and refuses to answer. You can teach it how to speak, but not to understand. In order for it to understand, the computer first needs to learn about context.

Computers are hampered by two linguistic phenomena: the homophony and the polysemy of words

Homophones are words with the same sound but different meanings, such as *eye* and *I* or *tire* (car wheel) and *tire* (fatigue).[11] Balázs Vargha[12] speaks of this phenomenon with appreciation: "Homophony is an inevitable feature of all languages—in fact, a spice well-suited for rhyming and playing."

Well, English has a bit too much of this spice for computers to handle, much less language learners.

I recently saw two teenagers in a second-hand bookstore. They were discussing the title of an English book on the violinist Ede Reményi: *Fly, My Swallow*. One of them said, "I know 'fly,' the

---

11. In English, some homophones are homographs as well ("tire"), and some are not ("eye" and "I"). The Hungarian examples are *ár*, i.e., "price," "current/tide," "awl," or "are" (a unit of area) and *szív*—"heart" or "inhale," both being homophones and homographs.

12. Hungarian writer, literary historian, librarian, educator, and specialist in language games (1921–1996).

insect, and 'swallow,' to gulp. But what can 'my' be doing there?"

Polysemy, the capacity for a sign (such as a word, phrase, or symbol) to have multiple meanings is the other reason why computers are better at speaking than at comprehension. It is usually born from extending the concrete meaning of a word to some abstract area. Think of *cuisine* in French. How will the computer know whether to translate it as "kitchen" or "cuisine"? Or *bottleneck*—did the writer mean the neck of a bottle or a point of congestion or blockage?

When there is a well-defined, limited context, computers are reliable tools for translation. In Canada, weather forecasts can be entered in English and retrieved in French. In this case there is no doubt about the interpretation of atmosphere, thaw, or fog. But I don't know how a computer will cope with the meanings of *pitch* in technical texts (a black substance, a throw [e.g., in baseball], the rate of descent, or the frequency of a sound). Or how will the computer select the correct meaning from the variants of *pile(s)* (fine hair, a pyre, a heap, the reverse of a coin, a stake, a hemorrhoid, etc.)?

It is easy to lose one's way in the jungle of vocabulary. Therefore you need to meet linguistic phenomena frequently so that you can find a way through it.

I have said many times on radio and television that books—which can be consulted at any time, questioned again and again, and read into scraps—cannot be rivaled as a language-learning tool.

In one of his short stories Dezső Kosztolányi (1885–1936) beautifully describes learning a language from a book. Some excerpts are worth inserting here:

That summer, my only thought was having a rest, playing ball, and swimming. Therefore, I didn't bring along anything to work with. At the last minute, I threw a Portuguese book into my baggage.

...once outdoors, by necessity, I resigned myself to the book, and in the prison of my solitude, formed by dolomite rocks on one side and vast forests on the other, between the sky and the water, I started to understand the text. At first it was difficult. Then I got the hang of it. I resolved I would get to the bottom of it, without a teacher or a dictionary. To spur my instinct and creativity, I imagined I would be hit by some great trouble were I not to understand it exactly, or maybe an unknown tyrant would even condemn me to death.

It was a strange game. The first week, I sweated blood. The second, I intuited what it was about. The third week, I greeted the birds in Portuguese, who then chatted with me...

...I doubt if I could ever use Portuguese in my life or if I would be able to read any other Portuguese books. But it is not important. I did not regret this summer's steeplechase. I wonder about those who learn a language for practical reasons rather than for itself. Knowing is boring. The only thing of interest is learning.

...An exciting game, a coquettish hide-and-seek, a magnificent flirt with the spirit of humanity. Never do we read so fluently and with such keen eyes as in a new, hardly known language. We grow young by it; we become children, babbling babies. We seem to start a new life. This is the elixir of my life.

...Sometimes I think with a certain joy that I can even learn Chinese at my ancient age, and that I can recall the bygone pleasure of childhood when I first uttered in the superstitious, old language "mother," and when I fell asleep with this word: "milk."[13]

---

13. From "Portugálul olvasok" [I read in Portuguese], in *Erős várunk, a nyelv* [Our strong fortress, language].

After this confession of lyrical beauty, let me say that although more efficient means of learning exist, more accessible and obliging ones do not. In order to have an hour's dialogue with a book, the most you need to do is amble to the nearest library. If it were as easy to get hold of an intelligent, cordial, and patient partner, I would recommend that instead.

I mention the library only as a last resort. Although its walls, covered with shelves, are a home and a school for patrons, I still recommend buying your own books for language learning. They can be spiced with underlines, question marks, and exclamation points; they can be thumbed and dog-eared, plucked to their essential core, and annotated so that they become a mirror of yourself. And what shall you write in the margins?

Write only the forms and phrases you have understood and figured out from context

Feel free to skip over what you can't immediately understand. If a word is important, it will occur several times and explain itself anyway. Base your progress on the known, not the unknown. The more you read, the more phrases you will write in the margins. The knowledge you obtain will be much deeper than what you will derive from the dictionary. The sense of achievement provides you with an emotional-affective charge: You have sprung open a lock; you have solved a puzzle. The word that has become self-sufficient will more readily pop up in your memory whenever you want to weave it into your own message.

Many people question the expediency of language acquisition based on reading. They may be right. I am a language learner by profession. I do not undertake the activity of language teaching. I feel like an amateur at teaching.

Amateurs are characterized by, among other things, not being able to transcend their own confines. A dilettante cook will prepare well only what he eats with pleasure. A non-professional seamstress will botch clothes not sewn to her own size or taste. I would like to emphasize that the method I have been promoting for years was tailored to people with the same intellectual build as mine. It leads to success for those whom I usually call bookworms.

The main attribute of this type is *not* reading a lot. Reading—such as devouring crime stories—is often nothing but an escape from reality: an intoxicant and a narcotic. Of course, it is still less dangerous than alcohol or marijuana.

But it is not the number of pages consumed per week that makes someone a reader; it is the ability to enter the pages of a book

A character's fate becomes the reader's fate; the author's style becomes the reader's style. The *plane* of pages becomes a three-dimensional *space* of reality in which readers, too, have their place. This is how the *inter esse* will function as a vehicle and catalyst for acquiring knowledge. Self-sufficiency develops, and the most expedient means of memorization occurs: emotional-affective tension. Genuine readers sail with Robinson Crusoe, throw themselves under the train with Anna Karenina, and die of tuberculosis with the Lady of the Camellias. Afterward, luckily, they come back to life.

I frequently emphasize the importance of books. I might overemphasize it. But books were how my generation became acquainted with the realities of life, and books were our refuge if those realities proved too stern.

Today's youth has been won over by imagery—moving, colorful pictures with sound. The light of letters has faded to shadows. The decline of the Gutenberg galaxy is often taken for some celestial phenomenon like shooting stars on an August night.

Images, words, and sounds have always competed with each other. Antiquity attributed magic power to words. Isis gained the upper hand over the Sun God, considered invincible, by finding out and uttering his name. The third commandment of the Old Testament—"Thou shalt not take the name of the Lord thy God in vain"—was not only a means to enhance the status of God but also a weapon in the fight against the Egyptian wizardry of words.

We, lovers of words, can be proud that an enemy is cursed by "speaking badly of" (malediction) and those worthy are blessed with "speaking well of" (benediction). In Hungarian, "taking things by a good or bad name" means taking them kindly or amiss. The magic power of words is evident when a prisoner of war suffers torture rather than give up information to his enemy. Perhaps it is not merely sheer recalcitrance but recognition of this power when a child remains silent when prodded, "Tell your auntie your name, will you?" The close identity of the name and its bearer is reflected in a beautiful expression by Anna Lesznai (1885–1966): "But once ever I find my name / My many deaths are all just dreams."[14]

Dezső Kosztolányi wrote, "For ordinary mortals, language is a means; it is an end in itself only for language learners and poets."

Great poets—artists—polish language into a shining jewel to place on a pedestal. Gyula Juhász (1883–1937) wrote:

"Words, wonderful words: / They appease and incite. / They rule over lives. / They haunt like ghosts. / They soar like thoughts. / Stooping, they bear worries. / They symbolize a universe. / You

---

14. *"De ha nevem megtalálom / Sok halálom csupa álom."*

are dead when they are gone."[15]

Catholicism was the age of images; Protestantism, of writing

Stained-glass windows of Renaissance churches filter sunlight, dimming eyesight; in any case the illiterate masses couldn't have read the prayer book anyway. And lay believers didn't understand the Latin words of sermons. It was paintings and sculptures that related the saints' martyrdom and glorification.

The translation of the Bible into national languages brought about the age of letterdom. The invention of book printing reduced illiteracy. Light poured in through transparent panes of church windows, and the common people learned to read.

Mid-20th century migrations fed the power of images. Immigrants in America—Irish, Italian, and Polish—were addressed in the international language of pictures—movies. This art form, born at the outset of the century, bloomed. The cinema's decline started in the 1960s, and I fear it will die at a respectable old age at the threshold of the 21st century. In the 1960s film was already being replaced by its not so new rival, television. Television's popularity surpassed all other success stories. In 1945, there were 40,000 sets in operation; by 1949, this figure was 4 million, and in 1959, 40 million.

What conclusion can be drawn concerning the language learner? A plot adapted to the screen is a *liber actus,* a book performed. Pictures take less energy to follow than understanding "letters only," which take effect through mental transmissions. The young are spoiled by moving, colorful images with sound,

---

15. "*Szavak, csodálatos szavak, / Békítenek, lázítanak. / Eldöntenek egy életet. / Föl járnak, mint a kísértetek. / Szárnyalnak, mint a gondolat. / Görnyedve hordnak gondokat. / Világokat jelentenek. / Meghaltál, ha már nincsenek.*"

which means that

The young are less and less willing to rely on learning methods that demand intellectual effort

I consider *inter esse* to be the prerequisite of successful learning. If I define being interested as the desire to know something new, I can't help but question the learning miracles promised to us by the advocates of audiovisual education.

Listening to the same tape or record over and over again certainly helps in acquiring correct pronunciation. One cannot underestimate its importance. Good pronunciation plays a major role not only in the active phase of language production—i.e. speech—but also in comprehension: the right analysis and recognition of sounds. The concept of pronunciation includes what the mouth utters as well as what the ears hear. But the most ancient and most human motivation, curiosity, is left unsatisfied by this repetitive torrent of sounds besieging the ears.

What makes theatrical performances so popular among the elite? What makes football matches attract the passion of hundreds of thousands? Both have the power of surprise. Tension and curiosity hold your attention. *Le foot* (football) can be compared to an imaginary Shakespeare performance where it is undecided till the last moment whether Othello will strangle Desdemona or have mercy on her.

Listening to cassettes over and over cannot provide this drama. This is true even if the eye is appealed to (i.e. with quickly shifting pictures). Therefore I cannot recommend enough that you listen to the radio frequently. There you will encounter new linguistic phenomena that will demand your attention more than a familiar tape or record, which may allow your thoughts to wander.

It cannot be denied that sounds are more attractive to the young than the printed word. We booklovers are sorry for this reduction in the magic power of print. However, the shift of perception from the eyes toward the ears may be advantageous in one respect:

The dominance of sound may bring back auditory memory that we lost on account of reading

Missionaries taught reading to illiterate aborigines in Australia. They read Biblical passages translated into the local tongue and had those about to be baptized repeat the passages. The aborigines were able to grasp and memorize 10–12 verses at one blow. Ethnographers claim that tribes that rely solely on oral traditions can easily remember 10-minute-long texts and can reproduce them flawlessly.

We civilized intellectuals mobilize our eyes and ears in acquiring knowledge. Our mind analyzes, and our brain stores, the words, word combinations, and grammar forms that we picked up this way. We cannot call them ours yet: A violin that comes into your possession won't truly become your instrument until you learn how to play it.

How do we follow the path that leads from knowledge ("I know how to say it") to actual proficiency, the correct and stress-free application of information?

Whatever we know needs to become automatic to become a skill. This process is facilitated by the method that I recommend so frequently: talking with yourself.

Silent articulation of speech was discovered by linguists. According to A. N. Sokolov (*Inner Speech and Thought*, 1972), "[the] only associations [that] will remain in your memory . . . are [those that are] checked and stored by the hidden articulation of words." He pointed out that every act of articulation has a hidden (latent) period as well, even if it is not longer than half a second.

Professor B. V. Belyayev (*The Psychology of Teaching Foreign Languages*, 1963) calls inner speech a type of communication. "Thoughts are shaped...in the process of inner speech."

Not only speech but also music can be articulated and developed in a silent inner world. We know from the composer Pál Rózsa that a complex, multi-part piece of music that he created lived only in his mind. He heard it for the first time at an international competition in Denmark, where it won first prize. We silently speak our thoughts in advance, even in our mother tongue, without being aware of it.

I would like to supplement the above statements with practical advice. If you plan to speak a foreign language formally, for example at a conference, do not fail to silently speak your message for yourself in advance, at least broadly. As an interpreter, I sadly witnessed many times when intelligent proposals by Hungarian delegates were glossed over or dismissed because their negotiating partners couldn't make out the meaning of their imperfectly improvised sentences.

2

~

I START WRITING in a new language very early. By limiting my reflections to basic, everyday experiences, I can avoid translating from Hungarian. I take unkempt, clumsy notes but I find time even on my busiest interpreting days to write something in my current foreign language. When I have finished scribbling in my notebook, I have no regrets about throwing it into the trash. I don't even bother to tear it up. So many languages take turns in my notes that no one would want to decipher them. (And because of the highly subjective nature of my notes, they would be uninteresting to others anyway.) I find my strategy worth following for two reasons:

Writing is speech slowed down

The word chain develops more slowly; the context that creates order can prevail more effectively. By the time I have jotted down the subject, the predicate will agree with it in number and gender, the noun will recall the appropriate adjective, verbs and adjectives will be coupled with the right arguments, etc.

In personal compositions, as in conversations with yourself, you can eliminate the fear of mistakes

I will take a detour here to where the mother-tongue learning of a child and the foreign-language learning of an adult meet.

It would be tempting to try to find a common denominator, but it promises little success.

According to data by psycholinguists, a child becomes familiar with approximately 30 new words a day from the age of one through the age of two. This high performance is understandable because he or she is exposed to illustrative instruction during his 10 or 11 waking hours. Yet it takes children six years to reach the vocabulary and self-expression that are required for the first class of primary school.

I ask, what would be the dropout rate for adults who learned at such a rate?

Speakers want to project their thoughts intelligently when they speak, and an adult's world is complex. If the maturity of your message is obstructed by the immaturity of your speeceh, then you may be stressed and therefore inhibited.

If you feel that you must speak like a native, or if you have a pre-existing lack of confidence, you will be inhibited. Inhibition may be triggered by an impatient educator or a fellow student who has a more agile temperament and can achieve more impressive results than we can. There are two medicines I can recommend for these diseases. First, take it as a starting point that the author of this book is wrong. Second, you are the best representation of your own language talent, which is real and like no one else's.

Students who cannot overcome inhibitions should confine themselves to well-rehearsed patterns, as did Miss Doolittle in Shaw's *Pygmalion* (musical adaption: "My Fair Lady"). Eliza Doolittle was able to converse only in upper-class English and only about the weather.

The gap between your need for, and skill at, communication can be bridged by communication with yourself—in speech and in writing. Yet again I go back to children: Their accumulation of linguistic knowledge precedes their speech by months.

Of course I mean *articulate* speech. Babbling is something even an infant can do. However, this babbling consists of sounds completely different from those we learn. Infants' range of sounds—owing to the underdevelopment of their speech organs and awareness of the world—is much more restricted and much less selective. It is not filtered by the need to communicate *specifically*. A little baby gurgles out of joy. The sounds that ring like heavenly music in the ears of the happy parents solidify the infant's connection with the world.

By the time children reach their teenage years, they enjoy blowing trumpets on New Year's Eve. The deafening noise-making marks their existence and announces their individuality to the world: I make noise, therefore I am.

What happens between babbling infancy and trumpet-blaring adolescence? A selection process takes place, during which every sound that goes unanswered in the world drops away, and every sound that connects remains.

They say that there is no French larynx, Hungarian throat, or Polish palate. Whatever the parents' origin or the language spoken at home, a child will normally acquire the tongue learned in grade school through high school.

The considerable role of schools in language learning is explained by the fact that every subject in the curriculum provides linguistic education. It would be helpful to put more emphasis on this fact in teacher training!

What pronunciation we have is not a matter of the anatomy of our speech organs. Then why, one might ask, is there such a characteristic French, Polish, and—unfortunately—Hungarian accent, that even in the case of foreign-language proficiency, will be spotted by sharp-eared people in no time?

Answer:

Our articulation is set by the norms of the speech we hear

Whatever doesn't comply with these norms has no communicative value and will therefore fall out of our aural memory. Learning to talk is actually learning to forget: squeezing out all sounds that are not known and not tolerated by our native tongue.

This intolerance is what we call the idiosyncrasies of a language. An adult French larynx, for instance, can forget that a word can actually begin with the sound "h." This is why a Frenchman will often pronounce the German *Haus* as "Aus."

The palatalized soft forms of consonants will reveal even the Slav who has mastered English. A Russian will often say "g" instead of "h" before some vowels. "Gedi, Gedi," I heard a student from Moscow cooing to his pretty Hedvig. A Spaniard can pronounce a consonant after an initial "s" only if he or she inserts an "e" before it.

It is interesting that established phonetic habits are rooted deeper and attached to us more stubbornly than any other feature of our mother tongue. Many a Spaniard learned German while a *Gastarbeiter* (a guest worker) in "Estuttgart." Others, in turn, returned from "Estockholm" with serviceable knowledge of Swedish. A friend of mine from Osaka translated Colette's works in a way that all the beauty of the French was in the Japanese version, yet she consistently pronounced the writer's name as "Corette." A Japanese mouth will forget the pronunciation of the sound "l" by adulthood, and a Chinese, that of "r."

In wartime, people's lives have depended on pronunciation

An American acquaintance of mine served as a reconnaissance

officer in a coastal region of the Pacific Ocean in World War II. It was vital for his unit, he related to me, to tell apart the Japanese, the enemy to be pursued, from the victims in need of help, the Chinese. They could not rely on outward features, in much the same way as Asians cannot reliably distinguish European and American faces. When the Americans captured a Japanese solider, they required him to say "leghorn." If he pronounced it "reghorn," he was taken prisoner; if he said "legholn," he was fattened with canned field rations and released.

We know from the Book of Judges that the soldiers of Gilead lay in wait at the places where the soldiers of Ephraim might pass to cross the Jordan River. When the Ephraimites approached, the Gileadeans caught them and interrogated them. Whoever pronounced *shibboleth* as "sibboleth" was hacked to pieces.

Today it is not a trap of language but hospitality that awaits travelers. Of course, travelers approach any place with peaceful intent. They do not come to destroy but to consume. They consume goods they did not produce: hotels, meals, and local places of interest. The memory of their visit is not preserved by castle walls knocked down; at most they carve an inscription with a penknife: "John Doe was here."

This peaceful migration is tourism. Its engine is curiosity; its fuel is brochures. I usually leaf through them with interest, even if I have no means of getting to the peaks of the Cordillera Mountains or to the Machu Picchu plateau.

If the brochures are about foreign countries, I tend to laugh at them; if they are about Hungary, I get annoyed. Those who produce them somehow cannot find a happy medium between dry facts and gushing praise.

A few years ago I thought I had found a refreshing exception to this trend in the inscription on the wall of Visegrád Castle. I will quote only its first two sentences: "At the foot of the mountain, on a somewhat elevated place, stands a superb chapel; its walls are adorned with mosaics. It contains an organ ornate with silver pipes..." At last we have learned how to express ourselves simply and elegantly! Unfortunately my joy vanished when I reached the last sentence: "Quotation from *Hungária*, a manuscript by Miklós Oláh, dated 1536."

What have you become, our precious mother tongue?

I think the problem lies in the fact that we are slowly forgetting how to communicate. Conversation as a means of contact is going out of fashion.

The first half of the 19th century is often described as *graphomaniac*—an age crazy for writing. Transportation was not easy, even for the upper classes, and so correspondence became all the rage. Subsequent decades were characterized by *logomania*, the era of conversation. Salons flourished, providing unlimited opportunity for the interchange of ideas, and they were later democratized into cafés. The bourgeosie in cafés contributed to the development of the Hungarian language. By contrast, peasants contributed relatively little. The nature of their work didn't allow them the luxury of falling into a reverie about the beauty of a corn poppy or describing it in song; their life and language were reality-based. But the more well-to-do had the luxury of time, and their café discourse contributed to the shaping of Hungarian.

We city Hungarians, thanks to our temperament, were especially avid speakers and coffee house habitués. My contemporaries might still remember when a multi-story tenement collapsed on Rákóczi Road in central Budapest in the mid-1930s. There was only one victim of the disaster: a young maid. Where were the residents of the building at the time, four o'clock in the afternoon? As revealed by journalists, three quarters of them were at some café or another.

Why do people today drop into coffee bars, successors of the cafés, only to sip a single cup of coffee? Are they that busy? I don't think this is the only reason that social life has become reduced to card games and watching TV together.

As an interpreter, I recently chaperoned a 40-year-old foreigner. "Can you play ulti?"[16] was his first question after I introduced myself at the airport. "No, I cannot." "And tarot?" "No, I can't play that either." "But you surely can play rummy?" "Unfortunately I can't." "You Hungarians never socialize then?" he asked, bewildered.

Teens and 20-somethings are of the same mold. Once they come together, the speech-supplementing begins. The only thing that distinguishes them from their elders is a higher tolerance for volume. A funny riddle was, "If the length of a ship is 30 meters, its width 15 meters, and the height of its mast 10 meters, how old is the captain?" Its modern version could be, "If the thrashing of drums reaches 80 decibels, the boom of the bass guitar hits 110, and the shout of the singer approaches 60, how old is the audience?" Answer: between 16 and 22 years of age.

Music and singing have always been a collective action. Songs dress up individual emotions into a more beautiful apparel than the happy or longing lover could ever devise. The Gypsy fiddler would strike up "The Pale Yellow Rose" in our name, and the prima donna would sing of the purple acacia instead of us.[17] But

---

16. Ulti, or Ultimó, is Hungary's national trick-taking card game.
17. Reference to a classic Hungarian love song.

today it sounds as if pop songs, as lyrically bereft as they may be, exhaust the discourse needs and capacities of the young.

Cheering for sports on TV replaces swimming, jogging, or gymnastics. Our teenagers use not only their legs less and less, but also their mouths. Walking and talking have fallen out of favor, as have wandering and wondering. Nor do self-serve groceries or department stores advance the ability to talk. In the ever-widening network of such stores, even a deaf-mute can procure one week of foodstuffs and one year's supply of clothes without engaging another human being in conversation.

My main objection to the craze of going to discotheques is that it destroys and demolishes our beautiful mother tongue. Musicians' hastily composed lyrics rarely reflect the natural beauty of language; they extend the short syllables and halve the long ones. They subordinate stress and syllable boundaries to the single-minded power of rhythm.

I don't want to cite examples; I would have to include the lyrics and the scores. And by the time this book comes out, no one will remember the songs anyway. But I am certain that pop songs are one of the factors in the destruction of our language.

3

~

THIS YOUNG GENERATION definitely cannot be blamed for speaking pretentiously. Wordy and flowery language started to go out of fashion toward the end of the 19th century, around the time when quills were replaced by steel pens. Bertrand Russell wrote that an introduction, discussion, and conclusion were mandatory in letters composed before then. The same was true of school essays when I was a student.

It may have been the appearance of telegrams and then telexes that led people to more succinct wording. Lack of time created impatience. In Western newspapers one can see eye-catching headlines that reveal the gist of an article at a single glance. Otherwise the eye won't glide to the text below.

I remember how the British press commented on Prime Minister Macmillan's historic proposal for the French-English détente. The most prestigious and most conservative British daily paid tribute under this headline: "OK, Mac!"

4

~

WORDINESS, however, is not dead, but sleepeth. What keeps it alive? Bureaucracy and its bloodchild, self-importance. We don't know the antidote for this malady, although its primary symptom can be recognized easily: *substantivitis,* the superabundance of nouns (substantives).

In the beginning was the verb, but somehow it went out of vogue. It was then superseded by the noun, and by neither-fish-nor-fowl verbiage appended to it.

Whoever tries to use our officialese to form an impression of the condition of our nation will assert that no one has worked here for a while. All they have done is to take aim, set an objective, get around to things, implement, realize, and ensure.

The following eloquent examples, broadcast on TV, were collected by Dr. Gedeon Dienes.[18]

The implementation of this program was realized successfully.

Procurement of groundwater is happening at the moment.

We will perform the transaction of the business.

Recently, when I was in a huffy mood, I gathered the following gems in a single week:

The conference will give opportunity for experts to exchange each other's (!) experience. *(Radio reports about an international teachers' meeting)*

---

18. Hungarian educational researcher, critic, and linguist (1914–2005).

Falls occurred on slippery sidewalks in the order of magnitude of tens. *(A traffic report)*

I can basically give expression to my conviction that it is so. *(Answer to a reporter's question)*

In the framework of the new psychiatry program, we still wish to implement several more establishments, beginning with several thousand mind beds (psychiatric beds). *(In an account of the planned economy)*

The new center was extended with plot-level sowing advice activity. *(In the lecture of an agronomist)*

Due to the receipt of goods, opening hours are closed all day today. *(On a scrawled notice hanging on a shop door)*

The answer to our question directed at the council was in the negative *(nemleges)*. *(In an official statement)*

This last phrase especially annoyed me, not only because of its pomposity, but also because the word *semleges* (neutral) has always been a favorite of mine. It is one of the finest words out of the roughly 10,000 coined in the zeal of the Language Reform (1770s–1872). A more adroit translation of *ne-utrum* (neither) could hardly have been found. By analogy the bland and insipid *nemleges* was born. I expect with apprehension to see its counterpart *igenleges* appearing in publications.[19]

I can put it down to the reduction of our linguistic sense that we coin words resembling firefighters' extension ladders. We convert a noun into an adjective, then into an adverb, then again into an adjective, and finally into an adverb anew:

---

19. *Nem:* "no," *igen:* "yes," *sem:* "neither," "nor," or (as in *egy sem*) "none."

ház-i-lag-os-an (in a home-made manner)

or

eset-leg-es-en (possibly).[20]

Japanese family physicians allegedly receive fees that are in inverse proportion to their time with a patient. Couldn't we remunerate authors in inverse proportion to the word count of their articles and books?

Let us give money to lecturers, speakers, and raconteurs on the basis of how concise their messages are. It would be a radical solution, but at least it would eradicate the *fiorituras* (embellishments) that may enhance music but make language tedious.

In addition to the superabundance of nouns, another disease has attacked our language: *prefixitis*. Our rich vocabulary of verbs is slowly shedding simple forms. I read in a police gazette the following: "Intoxicated, XY kept hitting and beating (*megütötte, megverte*, instead of *ütötte, verte*) his daughter. The neighbors called (*kihívták*, instead of *hívták*) the doctor, who from then on regularly visited (*meglátogatta*, instead of *látogatta*) the poor little girl and documented (*felvett*, instead of *vett*) medical findings of her injuries." We should be happy that the findings didn't get a prefix too.

I don't envy the miserable fish. They grow fat on corn that is "fed *in*" and in the end they are "harvested *down*."

It is less and less common to see a main message supplemented and explained by relative clauses. Relative clauses have been almost exterminated by the attempt to squeeze them into parti-

---

20.   In the above cases, *házilag* and *esetleg* would perfectly suffice. The first derives from *ház* (house), the second from *eset* (case).

ciples of the main clause. A contemporary writer would perhaps depict Miklós Toldi's great trouble this way: "sleep coming fluttering like a butterfly with drowsy sweetness on its dusky wing, but scarcely daring to light upon his eyes until night's being routed by rosy dawn."[21]

It may be the simultaneous interpreter inside me who tries in vain to cling to the lifebuoy of a predicate amid the surging stream of words threatening to engulf her. Let me cite two German sentences. The first I had to cope with at a congress. The lecturer's words were recorded on tape, from which I copied them verbatim:

> Von den grossartigen und faszinierenden Grundgedanken, die thermoplastischen Akrylharzen in Form ihrer, selbst in teuren polaren organischen Lösungsmitteln hochviskosen Lösungspolymerisaten durch die entsprechenden niedrigviskosen Dispersionen in billigen aliphatischen Kohlenwasserstoffen zu ersetzen, ist in der heutigen Praxis fast nichts übriggeblieben.

In the tense atmosphere of interpreting, I should have translated the passage into Hungarian. The result doesn't sound much nicer than the original. The English version could go like this:

> In today's practice almost nothing has remained from the great and fascinating basic idea of replacing thermoplastic acrylic resins in the form of solution polymers, highly viscous even in expensive polar organic solvents, with the corresponding low-viscosity dispersions in cheap aliphatic hydrocarbons.

All right, this mass of words was poured onto the heads of

---

21. Originally: "Sleep like a butterfly came fluttering / With drowsy sweetness on its dusky wing, / But scarcely dared upon his eyes to light / Until the rosy dawn has routed night." *Toldi: An Epic Poem* (1846) by János Arany, translation by Watson Kirkconnell in collaboration with Tivadar Edl; Canto Four.

the audience by an officious specialist. It may not be justified to expect from him an extremely high level of style.

But what shall we say about the following nested sentence, published in a periodical with a circulation of thousands? The journal, *Der Übersetzer* from Germany, is supposed to teach translators how to express themselves nicely and clearly.

Nachdem in den fünfziger und sechziger Jahren sich vorwiegend die Linguistik den Problemen der Übersetzung zugewandt und die junge Disziplin der Übersetzungswissenschaft sich in erster Linie mit von ästhetischen und künstlerischen Implikationen nicht belasteten Untersuchungen der Übersetzung von Gebrauchstexten und der Erarbeitung einer Übersetzungstheorie befasst hat, wird die Problematik des Übersetzens, des Übersetzungsvergleichs, der Beschreibung von Übersetzungen, der Übersetzungsäquivalenz der Übersetzungen als Rezeptionsphänomen und als unübersehbarer Bestandteil aller Literaturen nun von Literaturwissenschaftlern aufgegriffen und in variantenreicher, zum Teil auch kontroverser Form vorgetragen.

In English:

While linguistics predominantly turned toward problems of translation in the fifties and sixties, and the new discipline of translation studies primarily dealt with research on translation of functional texts not burdened by aesthetic and artistic implications, as well as the development of a translation theory, the problems of translation, comparison of translations, description of translations, and equivalence of translations are currently treated by literary scholars as a phenomenon of reception and a major component of all literatures, and they are presented in diverse, partly controversial forms.

I count 199 syllables in this monster of a sentence, which saw the light of day in a journal meant to *train translators*.

Oh well, we could say with a wave of the hand, it is the Germans' problem. But if we sweep before our own door, our broom will collect plenty of waste. Today's Hungarian style often reminds me of the popular Russian children's toy, the Matryoshka nesting doll. No matter how voluminous a modern Hungarian sentence may be, its message is really quite small and simple, like the tiniest Matryoshka.

Our inflated bureaucratic jargon imitates the German model. It reeks of the stuffy air of closed, dusty offices. As they say, we are a juridical nation.

In contrast, the Hungarian literary historian and linguist Tibor Kardos (1908–1973) wrote the following about the Funeral Sermon (ca. 1200): "Hungarian language with its vigorous ring is heard first in these 26 lines, but with an assurance that is not the least reminiscent of the tentativeness of initial sounds." On the other hand, we know from the *History of the Hungarian Language* (Bárczi, G., L. Benkő, and J. Berrár, 1967) that "Most of the extant fragments from Hungary are legal texts, known as deeds. They include founding charters, deeds of gift, estate and property surveys, wills, testimonies, and judgments." Béla III set up a chancellery and ordered that "lawsuits resolved at the audience of My Majesty be recorded in writing." Hungarian fragments preserve this "chancellerial" style. But the first intellectuals who started to speak Hungarian in the Reform Era[22] were lawyers or legal clerks (trainee lawyers). By contrast, the most an engineer would do was drain water from the fields; neither did physicians have any particular authority in society. Priests' sermons—even those by the "golden-mouthed"—lived only as long as they were delivered.

---

22. A period of modernization in Hungary between 1825 and 1848. Before that time, Latin was used for official purposes.

In 19th century courts, Hungarian was recorded by lawyers in thick, Latinesque prose. Written Hungarian shifted toward the vernacular in the last third of the 19th century when lawyers representing litigating peasants needed to simplify their sentences. On the other hand, lawyers also had to compose texts as comprehensively as possible and exclude all possibility of misinterpretation. The texts should be so that no lawyer with bad intent and a good nose could find any loophole in them, not even in 100 years.

I believe this is what makes our official language so clumsy— and, sadly, the only style considered worthy of serious issues.

In laws, resolutions, and contracts there can be nothing left to readers' imaginations. Everything has to be in place and in definite terms. This language is not like modern poetry, where you are free to (and must) guess what the poet means. In nonfigurative art we can enjoyably discuss what it is we are looking at: portrait, still life, landscape, etc.

But why do we express ourselves in articles or lectures intended for the layman with rigid minuteness that is appropriate to documents or court files? Have our authors and speakers forgotten about demonstrative pronouns, which are important devices in Hungarian?

When the Meteorological Minidivision of the Methodology of Metrology (in short, MMMM) holds its annual conference, the audience can expect that the speakers will use the full name in every second sentence of their lectures, not an abbreviation. As an interpreter, I can be nothing but grateful for this inheritance from lawyers. I can take a breath when I unfaithfully abbreviate the MMMM sea serpent as "This division." This sacrilege will not mislead anyone to believe that they have accidentally strayed into the Classical Cosmology Curricular Course (CCCC).

Of the parts of speech, pronouns are the best friends of the interpreter. They make it possible for words in chains, clinging to each other's tails like romping puppies, to be shortened into one syllable. Yet pronouns are fearfully avoided in official style, as are periods. Periods are the traffic police of language.

Those who formulate texts still view the period as a Trojan horse, which can smuggle an enemy into the carefully guarded castle of rhetoric.

I admit that when wording laws, resolutions, and contracts, unequivocality is a cardinal requirement. To ensure a lack of ambiguity, each claim must consist of a single sentence. But why does our educational literature, for instance, follow this convoluted style? In this realm, we need not fear the breaching of castle walls!

5

~

THE USE OF PUNCTUATION reveals at least as much about the character of an author as it does about his or her vocabulary. But punctuation is not only characteristic of an individual but also of the Zeitgeist. Julien Benda[23] spoke about the betrayal of the intellectuals, so let this chapter be about how punctuation marks betray us and what they may reveal.

The tell-tale nature of punctuation marks

When we speak, the message travels to the recipient not only by words but by stress. When we write, we have to resort to symbols that indicate stress. Punctuation (translated by Dezső Kosztolányi into Hungarian as *középontozás*[24]) also reflects the relation of the formulator to the message communicated.

Modern journalism uses and abuses punctuation. For example, one can rarely find fewer than two commas in a sentence. Quotation marks are indicative of a writer prone to wariness of the possiblity of liability. They reflect the stance of "not my department." Editorial columnists are often obliged to use them because of the nature of their job.[25]

Imagine that in the middle of the night news arrives about

---

23. French philosopher and novelist (1867–1956), famous for his short book *The Betrayal of the Intellectuals* (later translated as *The Treason of the Intellectuals*).
24. Compare *interpunctio* from Latin: *köz(ött)* means between (*inter*), *pont* means dot or period (*punct|um*), and *-ozás* refers to the action (*-io*).
25. Lomb is referring to the use of scare quotes.

political turmoil that has erupted in a distant country. The message is dispassionately transmitted by the telex machine and conscientiously received by the operator. Whether the cause of this turmoil was the left or the right is not known.

Then let's suppose that reports come in stating that an ultraconservative clique tried to seize power. Domestic papers will print the news as follows:

> In country X, "spontaneously" protesting "crowds" demonstrated against the existing social order. Country Y sent observers to the scene to clarify the circumstances of the rebellion.

On the other hand, if the uprising was initiated by leftist forces, the news will come to light in this manner:

> In country X, spontaneously protesting crowds demonstrated against the existing social "order." Country Y sent "observers" to the scene to clarify the circumstances of the "rebellion."

What happens if the uprising is in a country whose leaders we don't like but whose adversaries are motivated by sheer power? Will the story have twice as many words placed within quotes?[26]

Sometimes there are simple style concerns hiding behind the quotes. They enclose new words that the writer doesn't yet dare use without caution. In the early 20th century, *mozi*[27] (movie) was inserted into sentences by disseminators with an insiders' wink, as was *maszek* (self-employed businessman[28]) in the 1950s. Both exemplify the tenet "daredevils today, classics tomorrow."

Of course, the change exists in the opposite direction as well. Several once-natural, today-outdated phrases are increasingly

---

26. Today, of course, scare quotes are confined mostly to editorials.
27. From *mozgóképszínház*, moving picture theater.
28. Lit. those in the private sector (*magánszektor*).

placed between quotes. In the mid-19th century, elegant youths in salons were named *lion* in France.[29] Its Hungarian equivalent, *oroszlán*, was tamed into *arszlán*. Five decades later it wasn't used except within quotes, and today it requires a footnote, as does the concept it covers.

Words and concepts can become obsolete fast. I heard primary school children on the bus asking, "Mom, what's tuition?"

Literature has less staying power than its sister arts. No one but French majors would read Hugo's play *Le roi s'amuse* or Beaumarchais's comedy *La folle journée...*; the works are musty. But the operas born from these two pieces—*Rigoletto* and *The Marriage of Figaro*—seem completely present-day. Botticelli's illustrations of the *Divine Comedy* could have been born yesterday, but to enjoy the work itself, understanding Italian isn't enough. It takes the determination of a philologist—or access to a beautiful translation, like the one by Babits[30]—to do so.

The *apostrophe* is a bashful attempt to simplify energy-consuming clusters of sounds or to omit superfluous parts of words. Users of apostrophes feel they have declared war on traditions, but they undertook the challenge. It took courage—and the apostrophe—to shorten the article *az* (the) before consonants into *a*. In the 17th century, István Geleji Katona[31] said, *"A' Magyar nyelv boldogabb a' Deáknál"* (The Hungarian language is happier—i.e. luckier—than Latin).[32] In János Arany's[33] time, however, it is already with a deliberate archaism that Hamlet speaks of *A' hivatal-*

---

29. Cf. "fop" or "dandy" in English.
30. Mihály Babits: Hungarian poet and translator (1883–1941).
31. Calvinist bishop (1589–1649), author of an early Hungarian grammar.
32. He was referring to the ability of Hungarian to express "can" (ability) and "make" (causation) by means of suffixes only.
33. Hungarian poet (1817–1882).

nak packázásai (The insolence of office).

This form has since fallen out of use: the *-nak* before *packázás*. But the apostrophe occasionally occurs even in today's language: *Úgy megijedt, hogy majd' elesett.* (She was so frightened that she nearly fell—*majdnem,* "nearly," is shortened to *majd'.*)

The sentence-ending ellipsis is allusive, as if the user could say more about the topic but won't...not infrequently because she was too lazy to look up the details. Instead, she leaves it to the reader's imagination to complete the sentence.

As for writing, suffice it to quote Schopenhauer: *"Je mehr Gedankenstriche in einem Buche, desto weniger Gedanken."* (The more thought-lines [i.e. dashes] in a book, the fewer thoughts it has.) This statement doesn't apply to the Hungarian language. Hungarian needs more; we supplement the verb "to be." This verb—officially a copula—is swallowed in the third person of the present tense: *Péter mérnök.* (Peter is an engineer.) Russians insert a dash: Петр—инженер [Petr—inzhener]. Lack of a dash doesn't always cause confusion, but sometimes—especially in titles—they are essential. *Esküdt ellenség* (sworn enemy) is quite different in meaning from *az esküdt—ellenség* (the juror is an enemy).

The overuse of commas brings needless pulsation into the sentence. We also use <u>underlining</u>, s p a c i n g , and exclamation marks! more than necessary. Aren't we using them to ease the monotony of the message?

Conversely, semicolons (*pontosvessző*, lit. dotted comma) don't appear frequently enough in our range of punctuation, even though György Lukács[34] speaks of them in a lyrical tone: "I love the semicolon, which is neither a period, nor a comma; one must

---

34. Hungarian philosopher and aesthete (1885–1971).

feel when it serves to enhance a comma and when [it is employed] to diminish a period." (Citation by György Nemes,[35] *Pontosvessző.*)

It wouldn't hurt to popularize the colon. It attracts our attention; it can replace the conjunction *hogy* (that), of which there may be more than one in a sentence. For example, "The ministry ordered *that* care should be taken when systematizing data submission forms *that* their columns should encompass all types of animal husbandry." The second *hogy* now and then extends into *miszerint* (lit. according to which), instantly flattening the message into a file sentenced to die in the archives, tied up in red tape.

---

35. Hungarian writer and journalist (1910–1998).

6

~

MY HOBBY HORSE took me afield: I have ventured far from the gate of the castle of language, where six-year-old Hungarians have just entered. They will start school and learn consciously what they have known about their native tongue for years. Six is an infelicitous time for this encounter!

It will soon be clear that *big*, which the child has been using happily for years, is not big, but an "attributive adjective." *One* is not one, but a "definite numeral" and *many* is "indefinite."

In the third grade of primary school, children have to cope with words they have never heard before, not even missed. Their book speaks of substitution of parts of speech, sentence contraction, zero derivation, and the modifier of a verbal predicate.

They can't glance into a more attractive mirror of their native tongue even after finishing the eighth grade and proceeding, say, to vocational school. I wonder, is the text below (a verbatim quotation) intended to improve specialist knowledge, or the performance of our would-be automotive mechanics and iron-workers?

> In coordinate compound sentences, the relation of the clauses can be contrast, consequence, explanation, selection, or connection.

Will these workers need to know that an adverb has as many as 12 types, accurately listed in the book?[36]

Those few linguistic concepts that are truly and practically

---

36. What Lomb meant is not known; the types may include adverbs of place, time, number, state, result, company, manner, specification, and degree.

required for orthography don't justify the grammar instruction in this way (i.e. depth) and at this time (in grade school).

One reason that grammar is unpopular is that Latin terms were translated into Hungarian in an awkward and uncreative manner. In the Latin infinitive, we feel the endlessness of universal validity, independent of persons, objects, and time. This sense of the infinite is not really reflected in the dull and lackluster *főnévi igenév* (lit. noun-like verb-name). *Melléknévi igenév* (participle, adjective-like verb-name) didn't turn out very well either. The Latin *participium* contains participation, an active or passive involvement in the action. János Sylvester[37] proposed a nicer word for it in his *Grammatica Hungarolatina*, dated 1539: Let it be named *félrészvívő* (half-part-carrier)![38]

What shall we say about the subject and the predicate? As regards the first (*alany*),[39] I think Hungarian is more clever than other languages. I don't like the word *subject* (French *sujet*) in other languages. I feel subjugation in them; they mean subordinate. But actually they dominate and control, rather than serve, the other parts of the sentence.

Állítmány (predicate) belongs among the less successful coinages, as does *alkotmány* (constitution) or *költemény* (poem);[40] the latter was first used in the sense of fabrication (figment). Now I know that the Latin word (praedicatum) from which *állítmány* was translated derives from the verb *praedicare* (to declare), rather than *praedicere* (to predict), as I mistakenly supposed.

---

37. Writer, philologist, and translator of the Bible (ca. 1504–1552).
38. They partly ("halfway") carry the attributes of a noun (e.g., case) and partly those of a verb (e.g., time).
39. It reflects being under (*alatt*) other things, such as a base (*alap*).
40. -*mány* is a noun-forming suffix. *Állít:* claim, state; *alkot:* create, form; *költ:* compose, make up.

My mistake may have been caused by my trade, simultaneous interpreting. Sometimes we have to translate seconds before the speaker utters the redeeming predicate. We mostly get into a fix when the source language is German. In German the predicate is often the tail of a sentence serpent that reveals what the speaker means to say.

Here is a joke that is the talk of the town in Budapest: A compatriot of ours with some command of German was invited by a foreign acquaintance to a theatrical performance in Berlin. Our Hungarian fellow stated after the first act that he had had enough fun; he wanted to go home. "I can't stand these surrealist plays," he said. "We've been here for an hour, and I still have no clue what it's about!" His friend entreated him, "Be patient! The predicate appears in the second act; once it's heard, everything will be clear."

In general-purpose texts, relatively little difficulty arises from the order of possessive phrases or from shifting the most important word of a sentence—such as *nicht* (not) in German—to the end. But in technical work (and no one can be familiar with every technical field), peculiar word order can cause pain for translator and reader.

Luckily, literary texts rarely need to be rendered in another language simultaneously. Imagine the trouble an interpreter would have translating this sentence:

Mit störrischem Trotz hängte sich die schöne Helene, als sie die Nachricht über die Untreue ihres Bräutigams erhielt,...

The sentence can have two kinds of endings. If the last words are "bei einem anderen Junge ein," then the girl who learned about the unfaithfulness of her fiancé did nothing out of stubborn defiance except link arms with another young man. However, if it ends with "auf einen Baum" (on a tree), then the beautiful Helen actually hanged herself.[41]

---

41. *Sich Einhängen* (*hängte sich...ein*) means to link arms with someone but *hängen* by itself means to hang someone. Note that it's not until the end of the sentence that the full verb is actually given and the meaning is decided, depending on the presence or absence of that momentous *ein* (lit. "in" or "into").

7

~

AND NOW AN ANECDOTE to return us to the topic of grammar and its instruction:

A bicycle manufacturer once attached an instruction manual to every bike he sold. One instruction was: "One should remain on the bicycle by having the rotation curve inversely proportional to the square of the speed of forward movement at all angles of balance."

This definition may exactly comply with the laws of physics, but I don't think those who learned it could immediately feel that they were in the saddle. Despite angles of balance or rotation curves, all that could save one from falling over is proper practice.

What advice can we give those familiarizing themselves with a bicycle—or a new language—so that they can learn how to control it?

Well, in the first place, don't cling to the handlebars desperately (that is, to rules) and don't be afraid of falling over (that is, of mistakes).

Our teachers are professionally engaged in rooting out errors. That's what makes them educators. Really adept teachers, however, will quickly realize that it is not that much of a problem to skim over a disheveled sentence or a slanted word formation. Teachers should not ceaselessly polish student expressions. Be more merciful toward mistakes! The majority of errors don't come from ignorance of the rules but from the fact that flawless formulation takes time. Speakers need more time than what is normally allowed by the rhythm of speech.

I refer to errors that are politely called "mis-takes" in English: in the literal sense, "reaching aside." The educator Endre Fülei-Szántó[42] judges the situation well: "An inaccurate sentence teeming with bad endings, a vague whole that already communicates meaning, is composed sooner than the subtleties of its particles."

Where will learners make the most mistakes? Wherever the new language offers more options than the learners' mother tongues

Hungarians often make mistakes using *er—sie—es*, он—она—оно [on—ona—ono].[43] They find it difficult to get used to gender in pronouns.

Our mother tongue offers strikingly little selection of modal auxiliaries. This is why it is a problem for Hungarians when to translate "I have to go" as *ich muss gehen*, and when to translate it as *ich soll gehen*.[44]

We cannot match the French for simple, snappy expressions such as *Il peut et sait dépenser son argent*. (He has the money and knows how to spend it.) French, like Russian and Polish, differentiates between *skills* acquired through practice and *ability* that depends on physical circumstances or environmental factors. Умею плавать [umeyu plavat'] means that I know how to swim because I learned it. Могу плавать [mogu plavat'] means I can swim because my arms don't hurt, the water is deep enough, or swimming is not prohibited here.

Japanese and Russian people make many mistakes in

---

42. Hungarian language educator, linguist, professor (1924–1995).
43. Lit. he—she—it, but "he" and "she" refer also to objects that have masculine or feminine gender.
44. In English, the difference can be compared to "I must go" vs. "I have to go" (or "I am supposed to go").

Hungarian because they find it difficult to get used to the definite article, which is not a feature of their languages. It is a pity for them that they don't know that this article is an important guide. It helps orient you in the complex fabric of a sentence; it dissolves the rigidity of the parts of speech. No matter how short the "the" is (in Hungarian *a* or *az*), it can elegantly elevate any part of speech to the rank of the protagonist—the subject. For example, "The 'hurrah' filled the whole square." It is no coincidence that the appearance of "Homo *articulans*" indicates a higher level of human development, or that we speak of an "in*articulate* roar."

The cause of most mistakes in Hungarian is the "definite" and "indefinite" conjugation

I can recognize its difficulty when I am talking with Sergey. Sergey is a student of Hungarian at the University of Moscow. He speaks our language fluently, with a nice accent. His vocabulary would be a credit to Hungarians in their twenties; he has more or less coped with the pitfalls of grammar as well. He has spent a month in Budapest. Now we are strolling along in front of his train at the Eastern Railway Station, discussing definite and indefinite conjugation. I think it is a piece of cake, a veritable breeze compared to the unlearnable perfective and imperfective verb forms in his language.

Sergey: I don't understand why the verb is less definite in the sentence "I love a blonde girl" (*szeretek*) than in "I love the blonde girl" (*szeretem*).

Me: It's a misnomer. We should speak of a conjugation with a definite or indefinite object. The blonde girl is a particular person. That's why we need the definite conjugation *szeretem*.

Sergey: Then I should say *szeretem* in "This is the blonde girl whom I love," right?

Me: No, you can't say it like that. Because ... because the object of this clause is not "girl" but "whom."

Sergey: And what makes an object definite?

Me (flipping through a hoard of examples in my mind): The fact that it's preceded by a definite article.[45]

Sergey: But how shall I know when to use the definite article? Subway drivers announce the next station with *"A Blaha Lujza tér következik"* (The Luisa Blaha Square is next) and train conductors say *"Miskolc"* (with no definite article in front of "Miskolc").

Me: It's very simple! Because there is only one Miskolc city in Hungary, but many squares in Budapest.[46]

Sergey: There are many Astorias[47] as well?

Me: ...You know what, why don't we talk about literature instead. What is your favorite Petőfi[48] poem?

Sergey: I like (*szeretek*) every Petőfi poem. Did I say it well now?

Me: Very well.

Sergey: And is it also right to say *szeretek* in "I like all poems by Petőfi"?

Me: No, it's not. Because, you know, there is a possessive

---

45. In fact, definite objects also include some proper names (e.g., those of people, countries, and cities), which don't usually have an article in Hungarian, as well as third-person personal pronouns. Nevertheless, the definite article is a good clue.

46. In fact, the reason is that square names (such as Blaha Lujza tér) are used with a definite article in Hungarian (in contrast with English), whereas city names (such as Miskolc) aren't. The rules for the use of articles may be partly arbitrary in one language compared to other languages.

47. A major junction in downtown Budapest, named after the Hotel Astoria.

48. Hungarian poet (1823–1849).

there...[49]

Sergey: Oh my, how many things you have to keep in mind if you don't want to make mistakes! I've learned already that one should use *ismerek* for "I know every letter" but *ismerem* for "I know all the letters." But tell me, is *hallgatok* or *hallgatom* correct in "I like listening to Bach"?

Me: Well ... both are correct in this case.[50]

Sergey: Tell me, don't you want to go home yet?

Me: No. I'll wait until your train leaves.

Sergey: Thank you. If I ever see you off, I'll also wait (*megvárok*) until your train leaves.

Me (mechanically): *Megvárom.*

Sergey: Why?

Me: Because it's a prefixed verb.[51]

Sergey: So, if someone sees me in a café and asks what I'm doing there, I'm supposed to say "I'm sitting until my friend arrives" with *ülök*. But if I use a prefixed verb, I should use *leülöm* in the same sentence.

Me: Oh no, not at all! *Vár* (wait) is a transitive verb; *ül* (sit) isn't.

Sergey: Well, goodbye! The train is about to leave.

Me: Thank goodness!

---

49. The reason, in fact, is that "every" (*minden*) requires indefinite conjugation, but "all" (*az összes*) requires the definite. However, a possessive object (e.g., "his poems") also requires the definite.

50. The difference is only in the perspective: The first (the indefinite form) implies listening to Bach's music as a style or genre, whereas the second (the definite form) emphasizes the composer's work in particular.

51. The reason for the definite conjugation is that there is an implicit definite object, the moment of departure, stated in the subordinate clause. Nevertheless, the definite object does often co-occur in Hungarian with completion-marking verbal prefixes, such as *meg-* in this example.

8

~

ON MY WAY HOME on the subway, I reflect that Dezső Kosztolányi, who was rather pessimistic on the acquirability of languages, may have been right. "Can one learn a language?" he asks. And he immediately replies, "No, one can but study them."

I too am a skeptic about learnability. In Hungarian, some verbal prefixes express direction (go up, go down), but others indicate the completion of an action. Examples are *megtanul* (learn) as opposed to *tanul* (study). We all are aware of the difference between *úszott* and *kiúszott* ("he was swimming" and "he swam to shore and got out") and *tenni* and *megtenni* ("to do" and "to get done").

When I recall that Russian calls the perfective form совершенный [sovershennyy] and that the everyday meaning of this word is "perfect," I shrink from using it in connection with language skills.

Kosztolányi's witticism is actually in need of clarification. It should be corrected for our expectations. People who have reached a certain age (normally 13 or 14 years) and plunge into the sea of a new language are likely to run aground on a shoal. It will probably be perceptible from their pronunciation till the end of their lives that they are not speaking their native tongue.

Having said that, they can learn how to be at ease in the new medium, especially if they are inspired to invest more energy by the driving force of all studies: interestedness (or motivation).

In choosing a language to learn, there is a psychological factor beyond motivation: public opinion regarding the difficulty of specific languages. Can one language be classified as easy to acquire and another as unlearnable?

In an absolute sense, not really. (To do so we would need to collect data that would answer hypotheses such as "A language is more difficult if it takes more time to conform to its norms.")

What is our goal in learning a language?

Are we satisfied, for example, with understanding a technical paper? Or do we endeavor to be verbally fluent? Do we perhaps aspire to render poems off the cuff, with all their rhymes and assonances? But there is another important factor: the native tongue and the linguistic knowledge of the student.

A Dutchman will find French more difficult than German; the latter belongs to the same language family as his mother tongue. A Vietnamese will learn Chinese much sooner than Italian. These two factors—expectations and linguistic background—cannot be separated from each other. If all you aim for is *passive* knowledge, then basic similarity will help you; if you aim for perfection, it will hamper you.

Let me wander again into the realm of my personal experiences. I was once in a sailors' pub in Genoa. I had sought refuge from a sudden gale.

Italian seamen were drinking with their colleagues of various nationalities. With no common language, they were helped by good will—and several glasses of rum—in understanding their Irish, Japanese, Russian, and Polish counterparts. But when the Spaniards started to explain something, the Italians burst out in irresistible laughter. They found it comical for someone to speak a language similar to Italian but different.

While sitting in the pub, I recalled scenes that I witnessed more than once at zoos. Children admire camels, shudder from lions, and delight in flamingos. But children laugh at apes. Apes are like humans but still they aren't.

Similar but not identical elements of languages—depending on your mood—will make you angry or make you laugh. You instinctively rely on analogies in the new language. A Hungarian may have better command of English or French than of Russian or German, but he will remember *leichtsinnig* and легкомысленный [legkomyslennyy, "frivolous, careless"] sooner because these words are close to the Hungarian *könnyelmű* (lit. light-minded) in terms of their components.

The more widely usable a language's rules are, the easier we find that language

Such languages are more predictable and transparent. Italian is generally considered to be the easiest language to acquire. My impression is that Italian is easiest because in Hungary it normally follows the study of Latin and French.

Italian conjugation is rather complicated. Verbs have one of four patterns; to present all varieties, Langenscheidt dictionaries have to enumerate exactly 100 models.

Let's comfort ourselves with Italian nouns. Nouns that end in a consonant are masculine, as are those ending in "o," with some exceptions (*la mano* [hand], *la radio*). On the other hand, nouns that end in "a" are feminine. Exceptions are words that are of Greek origin or that denote a male occupation (*profeta, patriarcha, pirata*).

Russian has quite a strong correlation between the endings of nouns and their gender. Only words that end in a soft sign (ь) require you to look in a dictionary occasionally.

Italian is simplicity compared to *der–die–das* in German! Neither the form nor the content help you get your bearings in its jungle, aside from a few clues (*-ung, -schaft, -heit*). Even a man has a feminine nose, even a woman has a masculine mouth, and both have a neutral conscience. Logic definitely misleads you. It is true that a stallion is *der Hengst,* a mare is *die Stute,* and a foal is *das Fohlen,* but a girl is *das Mädel,* and a woman is *das Weib.* What grows from *die Wurzel* (the root) is *der Baum* (the tree), on which *das Blatt* (the leaf) appears in springtime.

You cannot guess the gender of French nouns by form or logic. In Russian and Italian, we become used to thinking that nouns ending in a consonant are masculine. In French, nouns that end in a consonant are often feminine: death is *la mort,* whitewash is *la chaux,* and mouse is *la souris.* Those ending in "e" are supposed to be feminine, since this is the suffix to transform masculine adjectives and participles into feminine: *grand–grande, lu–lue, amant–amante.* An "e" turns even boys' names into girls': *François–Françoise, Louis–Louise.* Yet *foi* (faith) is feminine, and *foie* (liver) is masculine.

My ardent feminism rejoices that "reason" is feminine in German and French: *die Vernunft, la raison.* But I am sorry that "charm" is masculine in both languages: *der Reiz, le charme.*

A harmonic alternation of consonants and vowels promises ease; consonant clusters stop the mind cold. In Polish, we are not happy to see *drzwi* (door) or *przyrzecze*[52] (riverside). The other thing that makes Polish unpopular—the length of words—in a

---

52. An uncommon word that refers to the vicinity of a river. It occurs more commonly as a proper name or as two words: *przy rzecze* (by the river). To convey "riverside," *brzeg rzeki* or *nadrzecze* would be more obvious choices. Note that some consonant pairs (e.g., *rz* and *cz*) form a digraph (one sound).

way actually facilitates comprehension and making yourself understood. By the time you are ready to utter *przedsiębiorczość* (entrepreneurship), your interlocutor will understand what you want to say even if your pronunciation is less than perfect.

In Japanese, too, longer, three-syllable words can be learned easier. Examples are *kagami* (mirror), *megane* (glasses), or *tamago* (egg). It is short words that cause problems: *shi*, for instance, has many meanings; *sei* has several as well. Unfortunately, the horizon doesn't get clearer if two monosyllables are compounded. Compounds create the typical form of the language. For *shisei*, there are still multiple distinct meanings in the dictionary. If you don't see the character (which is different, of course, in every case), only the context will decide which sense your partner happened to mean.

The difficulty of learning languages that have words that sound identical or similar is the lack of plasticity, i.e., "pallor"[53]

In three languages that are relatively far from each other— Hungarian, German, and Russian—this pallor is caused by a high number of verbal prefixes: the long string of verbs in German, such as *eintragen, vortragen, vertragen, auftragen, beitragen,* and *nachtragen.* In Russian, it is the almost endless chain of forms, such as вложить, наложить, возложить, уложить, отложить, and приложить. [vlozhit', nalozhit', vozlozhit', ulozhit', otlozhit', prilozhit']. In Hungarian, it is not easy to understand that *kifest* applies to painting walls, *befest* to painting window frames, and *megfest* to painting pictures. *Elolvas* applies to reading books but

---

53. "Plasticity" may mean the ability of words to undergo changes or have obvious differences. Conversely, "pallor" may refer to similar words that are difficult to distinguish, as pale colors are hard to distinguish compared to vivid.

megolvas is for counting money.

In German we are averse to word monsters, such as the nine-syllable *Exportselbstbeschränkungsabkommen* (voluntary export restraint agreement) or *Langzeitauslagerungsversprödung* (long-term exposure embrittlement), yet the mind doesn't recoil from them. Their elements can be simply attached to one another.

In English we have hardly more basis to deduce pronunciation from the written form than in Japanese or Chinese.[54] This relation is not simple in French either. In *queue* (tail) or *eau* (water) we don't meet any of the letters used to note these sounds in Hungarian.

We are not pampered by numbers in French. Ninety-two, for instance, comes from four, 20, and 12 (*quatre, vingt, douze*). Belgian French has given up such coinages and introduced *heptante* for 70 (in French: sixty-ten), *octante* for four-twenty (80), and *nonante* for four-twenty-ten (90).[55]

I have one more comment on numbers. In Austria, a movement began some years ago to break with the ancient tradition of capitalizing nouns and words used as nouns. Language conservatives had good reason to protest against the proposal: Written sentences are made more transparent by this simply acquirable rule. The language cultivators countered by demanding changes in numbers. From now on, let 33 not be "three and thirty" (*drei*

---

54. Examples of inconsistent spelling are: mean, clear, bread, earth, great, wear, and heart; loud, sour, soul, four, trouble, could, journey, soup, bourgeois, and Houston; home, more, lock, love, move, wolf, work, women, and colonel.

55. Literal translations of the French compounds *soixante-dix* (60 + 10 = 70), *quatre-vingts* (4 × 20 = 80), and *quatre-vingt-dix* (4 × 20 + 10 = 90).

und dreissig) but *dreissig und drei*, and so forth. (Most languages have a similar structure.) If common sense prevails over conservatism and the proposal is accepted, German will rank higher on the list of learnability of languages.

9

~

ALL BEGINNINGS are difficult. When you hear a language for the first time, the words seem to run together: You don't know which syllable ends a word and which syllable begins the next one. In Hungarian and Czech, the stress is always on the first syllable. It is helpful in separating words, but unfortunately it doesn't improve the beauty of them.

Our dictionaries group words by their initial letter. Nevertheless, the endings are more distinctive than the first letters. I recommend classifying nouns by their suffixes.

In English:

Readiness	Reception	Stupidity	Patriotism	Concession
Silliness	Exception	Velocity	Mysticism	Suppression
Happiness	Conception	Precocity	Colonialism	Expression

In French:

Terreur	Santé	Attitude	Sagesse	Rendement
Vigueur	Beauté	Magnitude	Richesse	Revêtement
Fureur	Lâcheté	Similitude	Tristesse	Replacement

In Russian:

Широта	Наглядность	Дороговизна	Богатство	Событие
Простота	Уверенность	Дешевизна	Преимущество	Прибытие
Доброта	Умеренность	Белизна	Достоинство	Прикрытие
[Shirota	Naglyadnost'	Dorogovizna	Bogatstvo	Sobytiye
Prostota	Uverennost'	Deshevizna	Preimushchestvo	Pribytiye
Dobrota	Umerennost'	Belizna	Dostoinstvo	Prikrytiye]

In German:

Prahlerei	Wichtigkeit	Ereignis	Schönheit	Reichtum
Schwärmerei	Redlichkeit	Erlebnis	Wahrheit	Wachstum
Wichtigtuerei	Eitelkeit	Ergebnis	Bosheit	Heldentum

In Spanish:

Mensaje	Servidumbre	Llamamiento	Honradez	Sociedad
Viaje	Muchedumbre	Crecimiento	Estupidez	Bondad
Paisaje	Certidumbre	Rendimiento	Vejez	Voluntad

This memory refreshment gives order to your vocabulary; it sheds light on the role of suffixes, indicating which are used often and which are used infrequently. On a lumbering train, it helps time pass; at boring meetings, it helps you pretend to take notes eagerly. If you find a partner, it is highly appropriate for conversation and competing.

I suggest that you don't attempt such a list in Hungarian. Hungarian is too easy for (native) adults, and stress always falls on the first syllable, thus signaling almost with a hammer blow that a new word is coming.

Unfortunately, initial stress is the only aid. Hungarian grammar is complex, the vocabulary is rich, and the range of sounds is very broad. True enough, we don't hide any sounds. We have 14 vowels; each has a distinct mark.[56] Bashful English speakers admit only five vowels in writing.

The structure of Hungarian sentences differs in many ways from that of other languages. When we translate into another language, we have to climb upside down on the ladder of nouns expressing a possessive or other form of genitive.

---

56. A, á, e, é, i, í, o, ó, ö, ő, u, ú, ü, ű. The latter 10 make up five pairs that differ only in length.

1	2	3	4	5	6
A feszültségmezők	változása	értékelési	módszereinek		fejlődése

The same in Russian goes like this:

6	5	4	3	2	1
Развитие	методов	оценки	изменений		полей напряженности
[razvitiye	metodov	otsenki	izmeneniy		poley napryazhennosti]
Development	of methods	to assess	changes		in stress fields
		("of the assessment")	("of changes")		("of fields of stress")

Because of Hungarian's different word order—I blush to admit it—I suffered ignominious failures at the simultaneous interpretation of Japanese and Chinese technological texts into Hungarian. These Asian languages link words in such a different order that the mind has to do several somersaults, even in written translations, to construct sound sentences. As a deterrent example—and partly out of spite—let me cite a Japanese sentence in the order of the original text:

[1]Standard [2]test specimen [3]using, [4]gas to [5]high [6]temperature [7]heating, to [8]room temperature [9]cooling, [10]core's [11]compressibility [12]adequate [13]or not [14]determining [15]so far [16]conducted [17]studies, [18]suitable [19]or not [20]ascertaining [21]experiments [22]we carried out.

In English word order the sentence becomes:

"[22]We carried out [21]experiments [20]to ascertain [19]whether the [17]studies [16]conducted [15]so far—[3]using a [1]standard [2]test specimen, [7]heating the [4]gas to a [5]high [6]temperature, [and] then [9]cooling it to [8]room temperature—are [18]suitable [14]to determine [13]whether the [11]compressibility [10]of the core is [12]adequate."

And this is the word order in Hungarian:

[21]Kísérleteket [22]végeztünk annak [20]tisztázására, hogy [18]alkalmasak-[19]e az [15]eddig [16]végzett [17]vizsgálatok, amelyeknél [1]szabvány [2]próbadarabot [3]használva a [4]gázformát [5]magas [6]hőmérsékletre [7]hevítettük, majd [8]szobahőmérsékletre [9]hűtöttük le, annak [14]eldöntésére, hogy [12]megfelelő-[13]e a [10]mag [11]összenyomhatósága.

Incidentally, it is much easier to translate technical texts and understand technical terms than it is to translate literary texts or everyday words.

I never miss out on visiting a marketplace when abroad. I like meandering among tents and tables as they help me get an impression of the life of the locals. However, my heart sinks at the thought of how long I would have to live there before I could explain that I want *crunchy* cherries or *rolling* raspberries[57] or that I don't want the product because the kohlrabi or the radish is *woody.*

---

57. "Crunchy" (for cherries) and "rolling" (for raspberries) are terms in Hungarian that denote freshness and firmness.

10

~

THERE WAS A TIME—very long ago—when the ability to speak many languages was viewed as a supernatural phenomenon, surrounded by the awe of respect. Prophets were occasionally seized with a "divine frenzy"; at such times they told fortunes and "spoke in tongues." It was possible only in a trance, in *ek-stasis,* since in *stasis,* the state of balance, one thinks in the present and speaks one's mother tongue.

Then there was a time—not so long ago—when the knowledge of many languages was surrounded by distrust. "Why does he speak French? Is he is a member of the gentry?" "Why German? Certainly, he sympathizes with the Nazis!" "Why English? Obviously he is an advocate of imperialism!"

Everyone is a polyglot: Even those who have never left their country speak their mother tongue at several levels, depending on their current interlocutor and the situation at hand

For example, suppose you notice an error in a calculation that comes before you. If the mistake was committed by a subordinate, you won't gently tell him, "I'm afraid a small detail was overlooked." Similarly, if the error was caused by the negligence of your CEO, you surely won't open his door and say, "There's a bit of a hitch, big daddy!"

But when we speak of polyglottism, we generally mean those who have acquired many foreign languages, possibly with minimal effort. They "soak up languages like a sponge." We revere them in much the same way that we revere a magician who conjures a rabbit from an empty top hat.

There might be such language geniuses in the world but I confess that I haven't met any of them. Even my most polyglot acquaintances were able to produce the bunny only by chance of birth, upbringing, or as a result of diligence heated by interest.

I may well protest against the existence of a talent for languages more fervently than the idea deserves. Yet I return to the idea now and again because people generally refer to it out of laziness: "I gave up language learning because I have no head for languages." I agree with the linguist F. A. Ibragimbekov[58] from Baku, who claims that talent for languages is nothing but a gradual accumulation of knowledge and skills. People cannot be summarily categorized as talented or untalented.

Successful language learning has several criteria, and they are not usually combined in one person at the same time

An above-average word memory and the faculty to acquire vocabulary quickly is the criterion most often cited. Because there are only a few dozen grammar rules, they can usually be acquired in three or four months. However, vocabulary is a boundless sea. We learn it as long as we live. Moreover, grammar is relatively stable, like money. Words are coins; grammar rules are banknotes.

However, this aptitude is not necessarily coupled with another requirement: good pronunciation. Sons and daughters of different nations don't take part in this competition with the same chances.

In Hungarian and in French, the accent is stable and very

---

58. Three of his studies are referred to in W. F. Mackey's *Bibliographie internationale sur le bilinguisme*. Québec: Presses Université Laval, 1982 (pp. 141, 432).

characteristic: Emphasis in the former is on the first syllable; in the latter, on the last. This feature of the native tongue directs intonation even when speaking other languages. We are at a disadvantage compared to speakers of variable-stress languages.

Of course, there is considerable individual difference even among native speakers in terms of good pronunciation—that is, the ability and *willingness* to imitate. The latter needs emphasis in order to account for an interesting phenomenon. I interpreted for excellent Hungarian composers, conductors, musicologists, and performers. I was surprised many times that these scholars and artists whose musicality was beyond dispute spoke with a strong Hungarian accent. I assume they knew the right pronunciation, but they didn't undertake the—let's admit—slight monkeying required to mimic the correct pronunciation of the language.

Getting oriented quickly in grammar is a third special gift. I have met people who captivated me with their native-like sounds and intonation. Yet I soon discovered that their vocabulary was limited, and that they displayed knowledge of only the simplest rules of word formation and sentence construction. Conversely, I have admired linguists who seemed to have assimilated the most arcane points of eight or ten languages and were able to perceive and explain the languages' nuances of style. However, when it came to conversation, it took me several minutes to discern which of their tongues they were speaking.

These scholars are linguists and not linguaphiles. A linguaphile, to borrow a definition from Nelson Francis,[59] is someone who knows and uses several languages and who learns languages with pleasure. Linguaphiles are not familiar with the vast, math-

---

59. American author, linguist, and university professor (1910–2002).

ematized world of linguistics. They just happen to have general good characteristics—interestedness, diligence, perseverance, and good memory—and are inspired by special motivation to dedicate their lives to learning languages and perhaps earn their living from their command of them.

Such people might be more superficial than others. The world speaks to them in forms rather than deeper meanings. They are interested in the garb of the thought. If offended, they will sooner muse about the correctness of the agreement between subject and predicate than realize that an insult calls for a reprisal.

A pianist is not necessarily a musicologist. A philatelist is not an expert in the design of stamps; he or she simply loves and collects stamps.

It is an unfortunate feature of linguaphiles that they cannot relish free verses, so fashionable these days. The sound of words is so precious for them that they cannot renounce the satisfaction rhymes provide. It is no coincidence that the line endings of folk songs harmonize. Not only rhythms but also rhymes dwell in one's blood.

11

~

AFTER THIS LONG DIGRESSION, let me return to my starting point. The criteria that comprise a "gift for languages" do not always reside in the same person.

The bulk of my fellow interpreters rose to the high standard required by the profession because they were given the impetus and opportunity to absorb a particular language from

favorable external conditions
particular motivation
an excellent teacher

The same people didn't go a long way in other languages. They just didn't deal with them. The duration and intensity of activity in a language is what is crucial, not a mystic gift for languages.

However, I think we can discover a common denominator among learners who achieved better-than-average results with less energy than others.

Children starting to speak their mother tongues and adults familiarizing themselves with a foreign language are capable of forming words and sentences that they have never encountered. What makes it possible for them to manage their existing knowledge—their raw material—in such a creative way? Answer:

Recognizing and applying the patterns in a language

Even gibberish conforms to patterns. Gibberish fills empty frameworks with made-up words in a way that at first hearing gives the impression of meaningful text. Its master—and as far as I know, its inventor—was Frigyes Karinthy.[60] An excellent writer, he was a superb linguaphile as well. He was able to view the vocabulary of our daily life with a fresh eye; he saw and made others aware of the soul of words and the hidden humor in them. His commentary—and those of his son, Ferenc—shed new light on idioms. The effect of their language cultivation is practically unfathomable. I think present-day Hungarian intellectuals can be said to be citizens of Hungary but inhabitants of "Karinthia."

---

60. Hungarian writer (1887–1938). This genre has been employed by other authors as well, such as Lewis Carroll in his "Jabberwocky" ("'Twas brillig, and the slithy toves / Did gyre and gimble in the wabe...", 1871).

12

~

RETURNING TO FOREIGN LANGUAGES: When you speak one, you rely on its patterns. The creation of new combinations of words and sentences is made possible by your knowledge and application of these patterns. I call this interpolation and extrapolation.

We interpolate when we use known combinations of sounds and words to produce new forms, never seen or heard before, within a language. We extrapolate when we rely on similarities between an old and a new language to blaze trails in the new language. The oft-cited "gift for languages" means how quickly someone discovers these connections, and especially how bravely he or she builds upon them. Accordingly I submit that

A gift for languages is not a matter of intellect but of character

I heard this from a swimming instructor: How soon children learn to swim depends on how much they trust themselves and the surrounding world. I am convinced that this self-confidence is a prerequisite for success in all intellectual pursuits. It may even play a bigger role than we suppose in the most wondrous human quality, creativity—that is, artistic work and scientific discovery. Survival in a foreign tongue demands self-confidence as well as openness, plus an invisible floating rope of interpolation and extrapolation.

Extrapolation between languages will be more successful (at least in passive comprehension) if the new language is closer to the old one. Interpolation within a language will be more fruitful if it involves a language that I call transparent. A transparent language has relatively few rules, and the predictability of correct forms is very high.

Because no natural language is entirely predictable, all learners will make mistakes

Kindergarten-age kids say, "I finded a big stone." They are unlikely to have ever heard this mistaken form; even less do they think, "The past tense of verbs is formed by..."[61] However, the analogy of *want—wanted, start—started* has a familiar ring in their ears, and they apply it in a new situation.

I have already described how a misbegotten extrapolation caused the tragedy of my life. When I was four, I declared that I spoke German because if *lámpa* (lamp) is *Lampe* and *tinta* (ink) is *Tinte*, then *hinta* (swing) can be nothing but *Hinte*.[62] The indignation generated by my silliness categorized me as without the gift for languages and kept me away from languages for a long time. This is why it took me a detour of several decades to reach this empire, whose paths I am still rambling with unceasing zeal and joy.

---

61. In the Hungarian example, the noun is irregular in the corresponding sentence: *Találtam egy *követ* (from "kő"). The correct form is *követ*.

62. A nonsense word in German, although this regularity between German and Hungarian does exist between words with shared Latin origins (such as *lámpa* and *tinta*). However, *hinta* doesn't come from Latin and the actual German word for "swing" (*Schaukel*) has no connection with either Latin or Hungarian.

13

~

NOW I WILL take a few steps backward because I would like to report on a language-learning method that has many adherents abroad. The "only listening" method, used in the Soviet Union and America, limits the learner's role to listening for several months. The logic behind it is that children are recipients of language before they are producers of it. The "only listening" method was designed for fulltime students in schools and courses.

The way of learning I propose is based on reading books and listening to the radio. It is for students who cannot be fulltime language learners.

A working person's lifestyle usually makes truancy from night classes inevitable. Every missed class, in turn, means a deficit and an omission hard to make up.

In addition, adults are not ideal students, in general. Age, employment, position, and the lack of prestige afforded to students work against them. What's more, adults resist learning lessons, being reproved for mistakes, and sweating for grades. Learning via books, radio, and perhaps video is better for working men and women. My method can be adapted to one's own schedule and it helps avoid inhibitions. Students using my method won't have to risk disgracing themselves in front of their juniors in age or rank.

The latency period in my method corresponds to the months during which a child is internalizing knowledge. Soon he or she begins to produce simple speech. The child analyzes and substitutes at a level corresponding to his or her intellectual level.

The following rule, from the French psychologist Piaget, holds not only for learning a native or foreign language but also for other intellectual activities: "Whatever a child is allowed to explore by himself will remain for life."

Our teaching methods don't satisfy _Homo ludens_ (Playing Man), who likes to toy with ideas and solve puzzles

Margit Kaffka—who was not only an excellent writer but a pioneering educator—wrote as early as the beginning of the 20th century that "Learning a rule may be emotional. It may involve enthusiasm and cheerfulness if a child is made to draw this rule from the cases presented. Creating rules from experience is an in-born human ability, as are eating, sleeping, or loving."

The short hours, rigid curricula, and large number of students taking language classes hardly allow for anything but a quick trans-mission and testing of pre-chewed knowledge. The hard-working students digest the material, but they find roughly as much plea-sure in it as a goose whose beak is stuffed with grains of corn.

Under such circumstances, can one find happiness by becom-ing familiar with a field and picking up its select morsels? For it is the one and only guarantee of lasting knowledge.

Perfect health would render physicians unnecessary; the mor-al maturity of a country would obviate the police; a sensible rear-rangement of the world would remove the need for armies. Let me add another utopia, perhaps not so hopeless:

In an ideal world, a teacher would be restricted to teaching how to learn

Fast-paced change and the conversion of knowledge to his-tory will lead us to this new role for teachers sooner or later.

But now let's return to the difference between child and adult language learning. Adults addressing a child will adjust their speech to the child's comprehension. Ideally adults should speak to children more slowly, more articulately, and more simply.

We might suppose that all beginning language learners are addressed slowly, simply, and articulately by their partners. Not so. My several decades' experience shows that native speakers can comply with this reasonable requirement for only a few minutes. Afterward they fall back to their usual rate and style of speech. At best, they will give consideration to our status as outsiders only by raising their voices and speaking a few decibels louder.

I am one of the jabberers myself. Even though I have never suffered more as an interpreter than when I was interpreting rapid lecturers, I am unable to maintain a slower rate when I happen to be standing on the podium myself.

It is important that every language learner should decide, depending on his or her temperament, when to undertake speech

I heard this principle from Professor H., a scholarly instructor at Waseda University, Tokyo. I had the opportunity to participate for a week in his classes for foreign students.

His classes consisted mainly of Chinese, Malaysian, Indonesian, and Korean young people, plus a few Europeans. However, the classroom resonated with the presence of the latter. I admit that their misbehavior made me blush for my continent. Unlike the quiet Asians, the Europeans attracted attention to themselves. They interrupted the lecture with questions, added remarks to everything, and spouted distorted Japanese incessantly.

After the first class I apologized in mumbling embarrassment to the professor for the behavior of my fellow Europeans. "Never mind!" Mr. H. replied laughing. "Those who blabber constantly and incorrectly will acquire the language in half the time as the Asians, who are so hard to get to speak."

"Won't it be a problem," I inquired, "that this uninhibited group started gabbling so early? Won't the errors be fixed into their minds and become as hard to remove as an inkblot on linen?"

It was good to hear from the professor's mouth the same answer I am used to promoting. "Language is a living organism," he said. "Not only in the sense that it keeps developing, wearing away, and growing richer all the time, but also because it has the capacity to regulate and renew itself."

An organism can sustain its balance even under changing environmental conditions: It will adjust itself to the new conditions. Thanks to the correct standard in writing or speech, mistakes will gradually drop from use, knowledge gaps will fill, and protruding, disturbing edges will be planed off.

At Professor H.'s splendid classes I learned how to learn. He never translated a single word into English (we are still in correspondence; I still don't know if he actually speaks this tongue). On the other hand, he kept repeating the same word in different contexts until even the dullest and dreamiest students were bound to figure out its meaning.

The modernity of his method is all the more interesting because one can legitimately raise this question in Japan: Why is Japanese language instruction ailing?

Everyone who has negotiated with the Japanese reports that you can hardly understand them when they start to speak a "foreign" language. "Foreign" is in quotes here because it really means English. In Japan, it is English that people do not learn well, whereas in Hungary, one can choose English, German, Russian, French, or Spanish to not learn well.

Lack of success is not a matter of effort. Japanese teachers and students heroically grind English from elementary school through college. The teaching of English has had a long tradition, dating to when the eyes of this country opened to the outside world.

I think the trouble may lie in tradition. The Japanese method of foreign language education was developed at the turn of the 20th century, and it has changed little since. It consists of translating written English texts into Japanese.

American interest in Japanese is rather recent. After Pearl Harbor, thousands of American soldiers were sent to crash courses. They were trained to become intelligence officers (or spies).

In addition to fostering greater connection with the outside world, economics motivated the Japanese to learn English, particularly after World War II. The island country was pelted with hundreds of sales representatives from continents hungry to export. In addition, thousands of Japanese tourists visited European capitals. Professor H. teaches Japanese to employees of English, French, Italian, and American companies, travel agencies, and large department stores. He uses the direct method, which has been known in Europe since the appearance of Professor Berlitz.

Professor H.'s method has precedents not only in Europe but also in the thickets of Africa and on the coral reefs of the South Sea Islands. It was the missionaries, those good fellows, who had no choice but to invent and introduce this method, for there was no interpreter among those to be converted.

In developed countries, we forgot or did not even learn the lesson we received from zealous missionaries. With variable intensity but invariable emphasis, the instruction in languages, including the native tongue, was built on the model of Latin instruction. Because Latin survived only in the written form, the one and only way of acquiring knowledge was by translation; assessment was done by having pupils translate. Translation, however, implied the unceasing involvement of the mother tongue. At such times, as Ferenc Papp writes in his excellent text *A Book on the Russian Language* (1979), "We use our stranger's knife, a foreign object, to cut into the living matter."

The mother tongue's familiar categories do not accommodate foreign languages; its patterns cannot fit the new forms.

Qu'est-ce que c'est? runs the first sentence of the first French class. A common, living expression, yet we must shut that pigeon-hole of our brains where the form "What is it?" is stored. The way a French person asks the question is: "What is it that it is?"

In our mother tongue, of course, we don't break idioms into their parts or analyze the origins of words. The latter is the domain of a specific discipline, comparative vocabulary research, cultivated by qualified academics and unqualified amateurs. Because I count myself in the latter group, I would like to fish a few out of the ocean of words for the purpose of genealogy.

Classical

What struck me most was the etymology of *classical.* It derives from *classis,* a military fleet. *Classicus* is something that belongs to a fleet. How did its current meaning evolve? Classical came to indicate belonging to a category. (The opposite of Classicism is Romanticism, characterized—among other things—by the dissolution of categories and the impossibility of being stuffed into boxes. That is why, as they say, the purest Romanticism is represented by the sea and its waves.)

Classical is not the only word that expresses the superiority and value of belonging to a fixed, well-defined group. The

Hungarian word *nemes* (nobleman) means belonging to a particular *nem* ("kind" or "genus"). A Spanish nobleman is *el hidalgo* because he is an *hijo de algo*, a "son of something."[63]

Character

The word *character* originally meant a simple instrument used for engraving. Its meaning today is an engraved, imprinted, lasting trait. The sum of such traits creates individuality. Its Latin root, *individuum,* is much more graphic. It means "indivisible" because an individual cannot be divided further. Few think of the fact that "indivisible" in Greek is *atom*. We use the word although we know that atoms prove to be more and more divisible.

An interesting individual may be presented in a film profile, a portrait. This word derives from the Latin verb *protrahere,* meaning "to pull forth," "to bring to light" (i.e. typical features). A caricaturist chooses among features and enhances the negative ones. Caricature is of Latin origin, too; the meaning of the verb *carricare* is "to charge," "to load."

President/dissident

The one who stands out from the others will lead the way and sit in front: He or she will be elected a "fore-sitter," that is, a *president* (*prae* + *sedere:* sit before). We don't usually recall that the opposite of a president is a *dissident*: the one who sits aside or afar. (I mention in parentheses that the spatial layout of our mod-

---

63. Or *hijo de alguien* (son of someone). Author's note: When someone deviates from the (respected) family lineage, the Hungarian words *elfajzott* (degenerate) and *fajtalankodás* (sexual perversion) (lit. behaving in a species-less way, *faj* denoting "species") apply. The Latin *genus* (race, kind) is not only implied in *degenerate* but also in *generous* (as if the kind or sort are trademarks that warrant excellence).

ern buses created a new type of human being: the outside-sitter. They are the ones who would not for the world withdraw to the empty inside seat. Let all those arriving later with baggage or a baby break through them.)

Ascetic/philistine

We use *ascetic*, which has Greek origins. It comes from *askein*, meaning "to train" or "exercise." For instance, those who exercise the right amount of asceticism (self-denial) will be well-versed in the world of the intellect. This is opposite to being a *philistine*, which is a variant of Palestinian. It refers to the city of Philistia, which was inhabited by a tribe in the 12th century BC. Its dwellers excelled in fighting but allegedly despised intellectualism.

The word found its way into the famous Hungarian graduation song a century ago when university students nicknamed stuffy burghers, who lacked any academic interest, Philisters. Philistines were also given the sobriquet *Spießbürger* (roasting-spit citizen, i.e., a narrow-minded bourgeois) at German universities. Hungarians followed with *spiné* (broad, skank, sleazy).

Bohemian

A *Bohemian* is one who despises social conventions and lives from hand to mouth. The name originates from Bohemia, whose male inhabitants frequently set out on a journey, roamed the world, begged, cadged, and related their adventures.

Ars

The Latin word *ars* is worth a paragraph. Originally it meant all human alterations of matter, craft as well as art (*művészet* in Hungarian). From this dual meaning, a double series of adjectives was born. From *ars* comes artificial and artistic; from *Kunst* in German, *künstlich* and *künstlerisch*.

It was also from *ars* that artisan derived, as well as artist, which we call *művész* in Hungarian. Hungarians use *artista* in a special sense: for an acrobat.

Ars was originally the opposite of *natura:* the two together formed the universe. Mihály Csokonai Vitéz depicted this dialectical unity lyrically in his poem about the shore of Kis-Balaton:[64]

> ...the timeless virginity of Nature
> and human Craft, this hero,
> look into the same mirror...

---

64. Little Balaton, the wetlands southwest of Lake Balaton. Csokonai applies the term for aesthetic reasons to Lake Fertő, an unrelated lake between Hungary and Austria. The excerpt is from the poem "A szélhez" ("To the Wind"), 1802.

14

~

AFTER THIS BRIEF and facile digression to etymology, let's return to foreign languages and the fact that we don't analyze expressions or rack our brains about the origins of words in our mother tongues. The reason we don't is that we all completed our intensive course as children and—according to our level of intelligence—acquired the language without knowing anything abstract about it.

Of course the opposite can be true. Many excellent philologists who move with impressive confidence in the most abstract realms of a foreign language need an interpreter to buy a streetcar ticket or order lunch.

Never have I had more convincing proof of the difference between knowing a language and knowing *about* a language than after World War II. That was when the training of would-be Russian language instructors began. The students in the course were recruited from two groups. One group was comprised of Hungarian educators who had already explored the language out of diligence fueled by interestedness. They were able to give an impeccable answer to every theoretical question, but they hardly dared to speak. The second group was made up of Russians who had lived in Hungary for a long time and whose perfect native knowledge immediately became unsure once someone asked the right way to say something and why the other way was incorrect.

Our good examiners—language teachers—did not appreciate this "merely" native knowledge. More often than not, the students familiar with the theory received better grades at exams.

The difference reminds me of an old anecdote:

A man leapt into a lake. Bystanders on the shore jumped in and rescued him. The suicide candidate, now safe on dry ground, shook himself and took to his heels. His rescuers indignantly shouted at him: "Where are you running, friend? The artificial respiration is yet to come!"

Let's admit that teaching the grammar of our mother tongue is a bit like erecting the scaffolding around a house already built, or drafting a blueprint afterward.

One of the reasons old, grammar-oriented language teaching was unsuccessful was that if you start speaking a foreign language, your speed is dictated by the rhythm of the communicative situation. The pace doesn't allow your brain to reel off all the rules necessary to find the correct form.

Running your fingers through the rules might be possible only when you translate in writing.

What lets you avoid mistakes is not memorized laws of grammar but the right form seen, heard, and said to such an extent that it has become second nature. The model, which rings a bell in your ears and you recall spontaneously, is a shoemaker's last, a template, a paradigm, or a pattern. Close-knit templates, well established by exercise, will emerge in your mind as if embraced together—or, in a more down-to-earth way, as word pairs.

Let's suppose that you're speaking German and are looking for the right form of a simple term such as "the beautiful roses." The mind is supposed to carry out the following operation (if it were a computer, I would say it needs to set up the following algorithms):

"The word *Rose* is feminine. The plural definite article *die* already refers to the number and case of the noun, so the adjective after it requires the weak declension. And now all I need is to flash in my mind the correct form of the plural nominative of the adjective…"

This complicated sequence can be omitted if our template— *die schönen Rosen*—has been affixed in our mind through practice.

In our language teaching, unfortunately, there is much more instruction than acclimatization

Perusing books frequently and listening to the radio diligently allow us to encounter the right forms again and again. If our interest gets our heart and mind to accept these patterns, we can recall them quickly when we need them.

These frequent encounters cannot be provided by institutional instruction alone. The little time allocated by the curricula and students' schedules is devoured by the translation of (alas, often bookish) texts, the explanation of grammar rules, and testing. Curricula cannot ensure the amount of instructional time that is—in my opinion—necessary to achieve reasonable results within a reasonable time: 10 or 12 hours per week.

A schooled mind—or a mind being schooled—isn't content with the automatic acquisition of linguistic facts. It also looks for the logic behind them, just as it does in other studies, such as history or physics. In language learning, the question is, which method do we use to untangle grammar?

A few decades ago we could have received an unambiguous answer to this question: Latin. Adherents of Latin instruction demand even today that it be compulsory—not with the objectivity suited to the topic, but with a repeatedly erupting temper. Among its keen supporters we can find representatives of opposite worlds. Latin advocates include Dr. Borovsky, an eminent professor at Leningrad[65] University, and Léopold Senghor, the former president of Senegal, according to whom "Latin culture is independent of skin color and is the source of civilization on all continents." Let me mention here that Mr. Senghor was recently awarded a great honor. For his literary work he was elected to the Forty Immortals of the *Académie française*.

In the pages of a book, an author can pursue a one-sided discussion with those of the contrary opinion. That is why I can declare with the bravery of a lion that I am against universal Latin instruction.

Let Latin be studied by all who aspire to become linguists, historians, archivists, librarians, etc. But as far as other students are concerned, I do not accept the arguments for Latin that are thrust by its proponents with the weight of a broadsword. Let's enumerate them:

Argument 1: Latin is the ancestor of all languages; the alpha of the acquisition of languages.

Counterarguments: Latin, as we know, is already a derivative language. If there was ever a proto-language, we should study it. However, even the fiercest classical scholars haven't exhumed a proto-language.

Argument 2: The knowledge of Latin facilitates the acquisition of other languages. For example, if *conditio* strikes a chord, it will be a breeze to learn the English (and French) *condition,* the Italian *condizione,* etc.

Counterarguments: This similarity does exist in the Romance

---

65. Today: Saint Petersburg, Russia.

languages. But even if Latin were as relevant as it is to, say, Italian and Spanish, we can still find a key to open the lock of other languages if we set out from a living sister language. We need not go back to a tongue that has been dead for a long time and that doesn't provide an opportunity for communication, even if this language is *Mutter Latein* (Mother Latin).[66]

I concede that Latin can be a starting point for getting to know the vocabulary and grammar of many languages. But let me cite an example from the natural sciences to support my position. In mycology, the study of fungi, we can find chemistry, physics, biology, physiology, botany, soil science, etc. Yet no one would propose that whoever is going to be a chemist, physicist, geologist, etc. should first study mycology.

To give a more prosaic example, there are several roads and streets intersecting at Gellért Square in Budapest. Sometimes we stop for a moment in the square: Which way do we go? We know that the top of Gellért Hill provides a 360-degree panorama, but we scarcely ever climb it purely for the sake of orientation.

Argument 3: Latin and Roman literature and history are organic parts of today's culture. If we don't know them, many concepts and ideas in our present-day life, literature, and sciences will remain incomprehensible.

Counterarguments: None. Greek and Roman mythology, history, poetry, and drama are as much noble fruits of the "golden tree of our better selves" (Antal Szerb[67]) as are the many beautiful tales and moral lessons of the Bible. However, I believe it is not

---

66. Latin is dead in the sense that its classical form is no longer spoken as a native language. At the same time, it remains alive in its later forms, Romance languages, with an unbroken continuity and an organic development.
67. Hungarian writer and literary historian (1901–1945).

Latin that is missing from the experiences of today's youth but Latinity. Latinity is a heritage of treasure that spans across borders of not only languages but also civilizations.

Let's make ourselves and others acquainted with Lucretius's magnificent words on love, Cato the Elder's wise opinion on old age, and Pliny the Younger's exciting on-site coverage of the destruction of Herculaneum and Pompeii. However, I don't think that to appreciate this knowledge we must memorize nonsense rhymes such as "nouns ending in *do, go, io* as well as *caro* are feminine." Nor must we rattle off *"ante, apud, ad, adversus."*[68] That's what usually remained in the minds of my peers after four to eight years of studying Latin, generally without knowing why the items in these mnemonics were lumped together. Of all the works by Latin authors, they can at best only cope with the boring Titus Livius.

The way to the flower garden of classical culture is not through the thicket of translations while sucking on a pen

Students should learn Latin classics by means of intelligently compiled Latin summaries, just as Greek summaries gave us a taste of the beauty of Homer's world when I was in high school.

Argument 4: Latin instruction is necessary because medicine and law are full of Latin words.

Counterarguments: For a prospective doctor to understand *morbus* or *terminal*, for a future lawyer to be able to use *fundus instructus* or *matrimonium*, there is really no need to memorize the highly complex Latin morphology and syntax. A linguistic or linguaphilic mind will happily ruminate over the five ways of ex-

---

68. A list of some 30 prepositions (presented in verse form) that require the accusative case in Latin.

pressing a clause of purpose in Latin. However, I hardly think that a soon-to-be doctor or lawyer needs without fail to know the exact difference between *gerundium* and *gerundivum*, or the accusative and ablative of *supinum*.

I don't believe, either, that an electrician must know that electricity comes from the Greek *elektron* (amber) to repair a short circuit. Or that only those who complete a course in anthropology can be considered human beings.[69]

Science and technology are full of terms that have Latin or Greek origins: *atom, molecule, ion, quantum, detector…* These words and others, which we Hungarians didn't bring along from the regions of the Ob River, will be increasingly common in our vocabulary.

If Homer and Tacitus were alive today, they would understand a user's manual for a stereo system more than a 17th-century novel. How they would like our television programs, I don't know, but they would certainly be annoyed by the fact that a Greek word (*tele*—far) was joined with a Latin one (*vision*).[70] Unfortunately there are other examples. The written form of the English word *computer* was combined with its pronounced form *kompjuter* to create the Hungarian *komputer*, misbegotten even for a mule.[71] What I see as a contradiction is that while we tirelessly eradicate international terms (trying to replace them with more or less contrived Hungarian words), there are still passionate advocates for obligatory Latin instruction. It may be that the same people who champion Latin are those who would draw their swords if some-

---

69. From the Greek *anthropos*, meaning "man, mankind, human."
70. Other examples of hybrid words are *automobile, biathlon, dysfunction, hexadecimal, hypercorrection, metadata, monolingual, sociology,* etc.
71. Luckily, *számítógép* (lit. calculating machine) has gained currency instead.

one says *konnektor* instead of *dugaszolóaljzat.*[72]

As languages advance, the endeavor to use a classical language as a model for learning becomes more and more pointless. A final argument:

Latin is a "thick" language

To unlock one of its sentences, you need to scan for clues—corresponding endings—with the vigilance of a detective. That is the only way you can match the modifier with its modified word, which sometimes hides several lines away, or the predicate with the subject, now and again waiting at the end of the sentence.

In strongly inflecting-agglutinating languages, it is only the agreement of telltale suffixes that help us in clearing up connections. Those who want to wade into this thick mire need to apply rules that, in terms of complexity, give diplomatic language a run for its money.

Languages evolve from the synthetic to the analytic. What do these two terms, not very aptly chosen, mean?

A synthetic form condenses: It bends and extends the stem so that it can play its part in the sentence. An analytic form solves this problem not within a single unit—with a morpheme—but by means of inserting separate words or with the help of word order.[73]

Finno-Ugric languages—including Hungarian—rely heavily on affixation. I have tried to teach my native tongue three times. I

---

72. Both mean power outlet. The second is used only in formal style.
73. Synthetic is meant here mainly as referring to inflecting (also known as fusional) forms, the most evident examples of this type, but it also includes agglutinating forms where word elements express semantic elements separately, although still within the same word. On the other hand, analytic is used here synonymously with isolating.

confess that I failed each time.

A British student of mine quit his studies of Hungarian when he arrived at the word *megcsináltathattam*.[74] He was unable to climb the steep slope of the synthetic form, being accustomed to the comfortable, analytic steps of his language:[75]

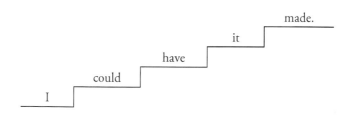

And so he didn't come again to classes. I feel sorry about this because I didn't have the opportunity to tell him that our agglutinative word construction is often clearer than an English word chain created by sliding several tiny words here and there. Because he dropped out, I couldn't have him compare these sentences:

Ebédet főztem: I had cooked a lunch.[76]
Ebédet főzettem: I had a lunch cooked.

I couldn't have him wonder at the elegant brevity of the Hungarian language:

"Shall I do her in or shall I have her done in?" (*Megöljem vagy*

---

74. "I could have it made." *Megcsinál* (make) + *tat* (causation: have it made) + *hat* (ability/opportunity/permission: can) + *t* (past: can → could) + *am* (first person singular "I" and definite conjugation that implies "it" as a definite object of the sentence).

75. The only synthetic element in the English phrase is "could," which incorporates possibility and past tense in the same form.

76. "I cooked a lunch" would be at least as good a translation as the above. "Had" is included for the sake of comparison.

megölessem?)

Maybe one day he will realize the beauty of Hungarian. Until that time I will rely upon the Word of the Bible: "Plead my cause, O Lord, with those who strive with me." For this sentence our language needs three words, rather than eleven in English: *Perelj, Uram, perlőimmel.*[77]

---

77. *Perelj:* verb (*perel*) + imperative suffix (*-j*), *Uram:* noun (*Úr*) + first person singular possessive suffix (*-am*), *perlőimmel:* verb + participle-forming suffix (*-ő*) + plural possessed object suffix (*-i*) + first person singular possessive suffix (*-m*) + "with," sociative case suffix (*-mel,* variant of the original *-val / -vel,* adapted to the preceding consonant).

15

~

FOR THE SAKE OF COMPLETENESS, let me relate the stories of my other two failures. After the liberation,[78] I was asked if I was interested in teaching a young Soviet soldier Hungarian. I was. But when he entered my office, a sign caught his eye: *Tilos a dohányzás!*

He asked me what it meant. I was able to translate *tilos* (prohibited) and *dohányzás* (smoking). However, I actually started to stutter while explaining the meaning of *a* (the). After several attempts and repeated paraphrases, Grigory asked me, "If not for the *a*, would the meaning of the sentence be different?" When he learned it wouldn't, he shook his head and stated that he would prefer to learn how to play the accordion. It seemed a bit easier somehow.

My third victim was a German girl. She was proceeding well until she became entangled with the distinctions between four verbs: *megörül, megürül, megőröl,* and *megőrül* (get happy, become vacant, grind something, go crazy). What other studies she decided to pursue I never knew; she didn't come around anymore.

---

78. The Russian army liberated Budapest from Nazi rule in 1945 while simultaneously occupying the country.

16

~

THE SIMPLIFICATION OF LANGUAGES—their progress from synthetic to analytic forms—takes place in some languages virtually before our eyes.

Complex, agglutinating, and inflecting forms are gradually dropping out. Let me cite a simple example.

Taught by teachers and used by writers, so-called simple past tenses (that is, expressed in a single word) are used less and less in everyday life. Two examples are *ich sah* and *je vis* (I saw) from the German verb *sehen* and the French *voir*. They are beautiful and elegant, but they give us a headache because they bend the dictionary form—the infinitive—in a way that cannot be formulated. That is why they are disappearing from the spoken language and are being replaced by *ich habe gesehen* and *j'ai vu* (cf. I have seen). Despite being more compound, these forms are simpler: They consist of the past participle, which learners must learn anyway, and the auxiliary, which is of course essential. These are basic elements of language, without which we can't even budge.

Once, at a conference in Berlin, I had to interpret for an English-speaking Indian presenter. "Was it difficult?" my colleagues asked me afterward. "*Wenn nur ein jeder so spräche!*" (If only each spoke this way!) I replied.[79] Although this sentence fully complied with grammar rules, it still evoked enormous laugher from my fellow interpreters.

---

79. The English translation above is a bit of an exaggeration. Lomb's usage was literary but not obsolete.

"Did you hear what the *Ungarin*[80] said? We should all *spake* like that, hahaha!" My expression was comical because it made an obsolete impression; today it would be rendered *Wenn nur ein jeder so sprechen würde.*

The antipathy toward affixation and inflection is on the rise

Even such forms as *Katis Mutter* (Kati's mother) are slowly being displaced by the form *die Mutter von Kati.*

This trend can also be detected among Russians, who usually preserve their linguistic traditions carefully. As stated by Dr. István Banó,[81] the use of the basic case of nouns—the nominative—is becoming more and more general in contrast with the other—oblique—cases. When shopping, we used to ask for "200 грамм (сливочного) масла" (200 gram *slivochnogo masla*; lit. 200 grams of butter); now it is increasingly more common to hear "(сливочное) масло, 200 грамм" (*slivochnoye maslo*, 200 gram; lit. butter, 200 grams). (Most often they don't say that, either. They just take it down from the shelf of the self-service store.)

The hard sign (ъ), which proved superfluous at the end of words, was abolished by Lenin with a single stroke of the pen. Verb arguments that differ from the general rule and logic slowly wear off to become regular. Чашка чаю [chashka *chayu*, a cup of tea], an exception, wore off to become regular during one generation: чашка чая [chashka *chaya*]. Of the two forms—short and long—of an adjective, the latter is increasingly displaced; its use lends a tart and formal character to the message.

The French language, too, evolves towards consistency. This

---

80. Hungarian woman.
81. Educator (1918–1987); author of the book *The Methodology of Teaching the Russian Language.*

is how we speak today, *Le Monde* writes (July 21, 1982): *Lucie, sa robe me plaît.* (lit. Lucie, her dress I like, i.e., I like Lucie's dress.) Breaking with traditional word order, the important and relevant part is placed at the front of the sentence. One can even encounter such sentences in writing: *Émile qu'il s'appelle* (Émile that he calls himself) instead of the prescribed *Il s'appelle Émile* (His name is Émile).

This form of manipulating the word order has received a nice academic name: prenominal apposition.

17

~

OF COURSE, the process of simplification in languages will not exempt us from learning grammar.

Thus, the question arises again: Which should be the tongue that can help us clarify the basics of grammar? I refer to fundamental concepts that are essential to avoiding mistakes even in our native language.

I have already admitted that I don't consider the mother tongue suitable for learning grammar. Facts that are deeply ingrained and seem self-evident are difficult to elevate to the abstract level of categories and rules. By using a somewhat flawed analogy, let me mention that everyone from Budapest knows where the Western and Southern Railway Stations are. However, they would be perplexed if I asked what their street addresses are.

If I consider drilling students in a dead language too high a price for learning the basics of grammar, then learning a living foreign language can be an option. A bridging language provides steps to another person, another people, another culture. The planks of this bridge cannot be as well-trodden as those of the mother tongue: In the latter, you don't need to cling to the handrails of grammar for the sake of your and others' comprehension.

I have predicted several times the polarization of languages. English and Russian will be *the* foreign languages for everyone not self-driven to be multilingual.

Of these two languages, English is scarcely suitable for clarifying grammar concepts. What makes English unsuitable is exactly what makes it easy to learn (at least poorly): the simplicity of its morphology. Russian offers a rich repository of variations: whoever studies the rules of this language will gain a solid foothold on the path of language learning. Its structure resembles that of Latin, anyway. I heard a colleague, retrained from teaching Latin to teaching Russian, incorrectly conjugating the verb *govorit'* (speak): *govoryu, govorish, govorit, govorimus, govoritis, govoryant.*[82]

On the other hand, the Cyrillic script deters many from using Russian to become acquainted with the ins and outs of grammar. I can imagine that many students would be unwilling to study Russian just because they want to learn, say, German.

In theory, a tongue that illustrates the grammar necessary for nuanced communication but which is entirely regular would be the ideal language to study. Of course, that language could only be a constructed language.

Let me present a question asked many times:

What do I think of a constructed language?

Well, first of all, I believe that a constructed language is a heart-throbbingly beautiful ideal. In history, linguistic difference—or sameness—has been used for the purpose of chauvinist incitement. "Language characterizes, but also divides, humankind," linguist János Lotz wrote. Breton in France, French in Canada, or Welsh in Britain are supported or artificially revived to achieve cultural or political goals. I don't think, however, that eternal peace would set in if humanity spoke the same language.

Speaking of constructed languages, Esperanto comes to mind.

---

82. The correct endings for the Russian verb говорить (to speak) are *-yu, -ish', -it, -im, -ite, -yat,* whereas the corresponding Latin endings are *-o, -is, -it, -imus, -itis, -unt*—the confusion is not without reason.

In the 19th century tens of thousands of people fought to earn legitimacy for it. Despite being an old-timer (1887), it is still more usable than its younger successors, Ido and Interlingua.

I don't want to refer even jokingly to the frivolous argument that we interpreters make our living from a Babelized world. Instead, I will tell the story of a conversation I had a few years ago with a female student in Havana. Once we made our acquaintance, the talk immediately turned to languages (I can't help it: I am just hooked on them). With impressive ardor Inés described Esperanto as the only salvation. I commended her and said that her effort was all the more praiseworthy because her native Spanish has many relatives, unlike Hungarian. "It is true," she replied, "But, you know, we Cubans are often smiled at because our pronunciation differs from standard Spanish—Castellano." (Indeed, it takes days to get used to the main peculiarity of their dialect, swallowing the "s" sound, such as *Yugolavia* and *miniterio* instead of *Yugoslavia* and *ministerio*.) "However, when this international language is spoken everywhere," she said with sparkling eyes, "all will pronounce *Eperanto* the same way."

Languages—like some kinds of wine—don't travel well

We tend to convert foreign letters into sounds that correspond to the rules of our mother tongue. The reverse process happens too, when foreign letters need to be altered—almost beyond recognition—for the sake of our pronunciation. The French refer to the Russian poet and his protagonist by the name *Onéguine de Pouchkine*.[83]

---

83. In English: *Onegin* by Pushkin. The Hungarian version requires even more letter changes, although perhaps arriving at a closer approximation to the original pronunciation: Puskin: Anyegin.

In our world built on television and radio, it is a diminishing danger that the pronunciation of an international language will be cut into splinters by the phonetic norms of national languages, much as we now have to speak about British English, American English, and Indian English. Maybe Esperanto will progress over time from affixation toward analytic. I can imagine that

Esperanto will be the language that clarifies the most important concepts of grammar

Writer Sándor Márai noted in his *Diary*, "Without a common language there is no Europe, only nations that hate one another in forty languages."

May Esperanto mean understanding and cooperation in the face of the specter of destruction! If nuclear weapons were to detonate again, they would destroy humankind, speaking a language not of hope (which Esperanto is) but of despair ("Desperanto," as Professor Walter Hallstein[84] once put it).

---

84. German academic, diplomat, and politician, one of the founding fathers of the European Union (1901–1982).

18

~

NATIONAL LANGUAGES and world languages are more than a stiff and rigid tangle of orders and prohibitions. Language is a tool used by everyone according to their need and ability.

I have written several times that language is the only thing worth knowing even poorly.

In physics and mathematics, a half-truth is not half of the truth but 100% wrong. Propagation of half-truths is not an advancement of science but a hindrance. For the language learner, however, it would be a pity to fall silent because he or she doesn't know with certainty whether a form will hit home or not.

To overcome such inhibitions, living in the target country has indisputable advantages. If you are there and don't want to miss the train or spend the night under a bridge, you have to ask for information or look for a room in the best language you can muster. However, the lack of traveling is often used to conceal the laziness of some language learners ("Needless to say, if I could go there…").

When you are abroad—especially as a tourist—it is rather difficult to make the acquaintance of someone patient, intelligent, and available enough to help you practice your foreign language skills. With the energy it requires, one can normally achieve the same results while staying at home.

I wrote in one of my books[85] that in Beijing I squeezed myself

---

85. *Egy tolmács a világ körül* [An interpreter around the world]. Budapest: Gondolat, 1979.

into a dentist's chair (it was not sized for European physiques) just for the opportunity to chat a bit in Chinese. In another country, I almost had myself initiated—for the sake of practicing English— into a religious group.

Here is what happened in Tonga, in the heart of Black Asia, in King Tupou's empire.[86] The thin English-American community of the capital, Nuku'alofa, assembled for Sunday afternoon worship: diplomats, language teachers, and sales reps. There might have been around 15 of us sitting in the small church in the yard of the royal palace. We were listening to the sermon of the Wesleyan priest in his beautiful, clear English. His last words, however, caused some embarrassing surprise. "I see four new faces in the pews," he said. "As is our custom, now I ask them to step forward and tell us what made them believers of Wesley's doctrines."

A young man stood up first. He related that he had given up his former hippie lifestyle thanks to divine inspiration and became a follower of the Wesleyan religion. Then an elderly man raised his hand. He claimed to be a missionary who interrupted his preaching tour in order to listen to the Word. The third was an English naval officer dressed in white. His ship had put in near Nuku'alofa; thence he came to spend Sunday among his compatriots. He was such a strapping, fine figure of a man that I thought, if I were 50 years younger, I could well imagine a religious debate with him— tête-à-tête.

In the end—no matter how small I tried to make myself in the pew—it was my turn. I stood up and said I was a Hungarian tourist. "Never have we seen such a thing!" many said in one way or another.

---

86. Tonga belongs to Polynesia (in the Pacific Ocean), not far from Melanesia, which means "Black Islands" in Greek.

I said that even though I was deeply impressed by Wesley's doctrines, some details were not quite clear to me. But the members of the congregation practically competed with each other to receive me in their homes and supplement my missing knowledge. What is more, when they felt, at the end of my stay, that I wasn't entirely convinced that their faith was the one and only way of salvation, they asked for permission to take me to the airport and use the time before my flight to dispel my doubts.

My knowledge of English grew nicely, but I don't think I will ever benefit from the fact that I am currently the most thorough expert on Wesley's doctrines in Hungary.

19

~

I NOW RETURN to inhibitions: You mustn't be silenced when you are unsure of the plural of a noun (for example, время, *vremya*, time). It would be a mistake to interrupt beginners by making constant corrections, such as when they say "have had" but the linguistic norm prescribes "had had." Believe me, the edifice of the English language will not collapse from confusing these two columns of conjugation.

We don't interrupt babies because of imperfect pronunciation.[87] At the age of one and a half, they may say, "Mommy give Baby candy!" By the time they go to school, their vocabulary and sentence-construction ability are limited only in quantity; in terms of quality, it follows the norms of their mother tongue.

Let's not be angry with mistakes. Many correct solutions, even stellar inventions, were born from them. Christopher Columbus's mainland, which he assumed to be India, was America. It doesn't detract from the beauty of the tale of John the Valiant[88] that the poet placed India somewhere near France.[89] Neither does the non-existent Bohemian sea detract from Shakespeare's brilliance.

Lapsology is the study of slips. One of its branches specifically investigates the causes of mistakes in foreign languages. A

---

87. A Hungarian example appears in the original, a ditty for practicing how to roll r's (in the Scottish way): *Répa, retek, mogyoró, korán reggel ritkán rikkant a rigó.* (Carrot, radish, peanut; blackbirds rarely cry out in the early morning.)
88. A Hungarian epic poem written in 1845 by Sándor Petőfi, translated into English by John Ridland in 1999.
89. It may well serve to enhance the poem's character as a fairy tale.

significant cause of mistakes is the lack of a holistic approach in language learning. The goal of modern mathematics education is to teach children how to speak mathematics and enable them to figure out the rules of this special language. It is only in language learning that pedagogy doesn't recognize the legitimacy of starting from intact texts. When advocating the benefits of intact texts, I go back to my fixed idea, which is that there are benefits of becoming acquainted with a language passively. This language knowledge can be activated later by reading.

Texts of general-interest books and articles are natural; they are not limited to the meager vocabulary of beginning textbooks. They speak to the normal reader. The great variety of books and articles gives us the luxury of choosing one that suits our interests or relates to our profession or hobby. These texts are reliable because they don't use the artificial language of textbooks. They are dynamic because no simplification breaks the whole into colorless and odorless particles.

Language is not a set of words. It is a set of prefabricated blocks that we use to construct meaning. Just as workers construct buildings using prefabricated blocks rather than individual bricks, we construct sentences using premade forms. We forget that these forms are often figurative, not literal.

For example, what dastardly villain would threaten his neighbors with death? I, and you, he, she — in fact, all of us! In all fairness, we do apologize for the atrocity of, God forbid, interrupting others. I woke up to the comicality of this discourse convention when I first heard this Russian phrase: извините, что я Вас перебью [izvinite, shto ya Vas pereb'yu]. (Literally, "I am sorry to break you apart [or kill you].") Then I realized that Hungarian, German, and English are no more merciful in their phrasings.

One "tears them in two" (Hungarian *félbeszakít*), "breaks them under" (German *unterbrechen*), and "breaks them apart" ("interrupt," cf. *interrumpere* in Latin).

When I began to learn Spanish (I admit, with my locks already gray), I had a hearty laugh at the term *desayuno* (breakfast, but it literally means unhungrification), even though the French *déjeuner*, which I had known and used for years, means the same thing.

Let's put our own (Hungarian) house in order first. My mother tongue has borrowed plenty of linguistic oddities as well. The following nouns are always neutral:

kellem (appeal)
jellem (one's character)
szellem (intellect)

They may imply that something is excellent, bad, or below average. But once we make adjectives out of them, the words will gain unambiguously positive connotations:

kellemes (pleasant)
jellemes (of strong character)
szellemes (witty)

Those who react more impatiently than average are *ideges* (irritable, lit. nervous)—although everybody has nerves (*ideg*). As a matter of fact, we should find this adjective as comical as Frigyes Karinthy's description of a person who complained about his "circulation" and "bilateral car-hearing."[90] It may be by the analogy

---

90. From the short story "Mint vélgaban."

of *cukros* (lit. sugary, originally: *cukorbeteg*, sugar-sick) for diabetic patients that we say that a grandmother is *születs* ("jointy," i.e., with arthritis), the brother-in-law is *epés* ("biley," i.e., bilious), and so on.

Hungarian is so flexible and pictorial that it can create numerous words from parts of the body. A Hungarian can be:

backboney (*gerinces* upright, honest)
mouthy (*szájas* lippy)
laryngeal (*gőgös* haughty, cf. *gége* larynx)
throaty (*torkos* gluttonous)
tonguey (*nyelves* pert)
fisty (*markos* brawny)
fitted to the eyes (*szemrevaló* comely)
bloody (*vérmes* full-blooded, sanguine)
faceless (*arcátlan* cheeky, impudent)
a belly-spider (*haspók* a glutton)
of carved ears (*vájtfülű* sharp-eared)
etc.

If they are "necky" (*nyakas* headstrong), they will not "back down" (*meghátrál* back off) nor will they "blink the eyes" (*szemet huny* turn a blind eye) to the "heady ones" (*fejesek* big shots). Instead, they will "stand onto their heels" (*sarkára áll* put their foot down) and "sole out" their truth (*kitalpal* vindicate their rights), no matter if they have to "act footlessly" (*lábatlankodik* be underfoot) "to the neck and the head" (*nyakra-főre* indiscriminately) and "elbow" (*könyökölni* push forward) for this purpose.

People who are "biley" (*epés* bilious) or "bad-livered" (*rosszmájú* malicious) will "kidney out" (*kiveséz* discuss critically) a friend if they "nose" him (*megorrol* resent sb); whereas a "hearty" (*szívélyes* affable) person will "shoulder" him (*vállal* commit oneself to sb) without "back" (*hátsó* ulterior) motives and they will even "arm him up" (*felkarol* take sb under one's wing) and "hand" for him (*kezeskedik* vouch for sb, cf. *kéz* hand).

Whoever is "eyeish" (*szemes* sharp) and "gives an ear" to things (*odafülel* listens carefully) will be able to answer "toothy" (*fogas* thorny) questions that "were spun on fingernails" (*körmönfont* artful) if they "hair" to them a little (*hajaz* have an inkling of sth).

The list of expressions doesn't stop here; feel free to play with those you hear.

20

~

LET ME HAVE ANOTHER WORD about reading co-
herent texts. I will begin with vocabulary.

It is not individual words that are the most difficult to remem-
ber, but arguments whose logic is different from what is usual in our
mother tongue

Russians are not jealous "of" someone but "towards" someone
(ревновать к кому-либо, revnovat' k komu-libo[91]), and they are
not envious "of" the more fortunate but "to" them (завидовать
кому-либо, zavidovat' komu-libo). If she does say yes to him,
he will not marry the girl but "on the girl" (жениться на ком,
zhenit'sya na kom).

In Spanish, one thinks "in" something (*pensar en*), is afraid
"to" something (*tener miedo a*), and feels antipathy "toward"
someone (*antipatia hacia*). In French "It's nice of you" is *c'est gen-*
til à Vous—it's nice "to" you. "Resisting temptation" in English is
resisting "to" it in Hungarian.

Let's take the verb "to (day)dream." Pop singer Katalin
Karády's hit "What Does the Girl Dream Of"[92] is also popular
in France, its title being "What Does the Girl Dream *To*" (*À quoi*
rêve...). "I dreamed of you" in Russian is "You got dreamed to

---

91. либо [libo] remains unchanged throughout the declension, as opposed to
кто [kto], which reflects the grammatical case.
92. Katalin Karády: Hungarian actress, singer, and sex symbol (1910–1990).
The quote is from *Holdvilágos éjszakán* "Moonlight Night" (lyrics by Mihály
Eisemann).

me" (ты мне снилась, ty mne snilas').[93]

Professor Context patiently teaches us how to avoid such traps

The same reality surrounds us all, but languages slice it differently. "Sea" is translated into German as *Meer* if we are talking about a body of water that is landlocked: *das Schwarze Meer* (the Black Sea) and *das Rote Meer* (the Red Sea). If a body of water is a subset of an ocean, it is not a *Meer* anymore but a *See: die Nordsee* (the North Sea) and *die Ostsee* (the Baltic Sea). However, a *See* is also what we call a lake, but is masculine in that case: *der Plattensee* (Lake Balaton, Hungary) and *der Genfer See* (Lake Geneva).

Laut, *Ton*, and *Stimme* in German (cf. sound, tone, and voice) can be translated into Hungarian only as *hang*. The generic, non-gender-specific concept of a brother or sister (*testvér* in Hungarian) is missing from most languages. The English word sibling is comparable to the nice old Hungarian word *egyfészekalja* (brood, lit. the bottom of one nest). Relationships that imply age (*nővér/húg*, elder/younger sister; *báty/öcs*, elder/younger brother) can be expressed only by clumsy circumlocutions in most languages. Russian distinguishes between in-laws on the basis of whether they are parents of the wife (теща/тесть, teshcha/test') or the husband (свекровь/свекор, svekrov'/svekor).

Categorization by gender is just as unknown in English as it is in Hungarian. Practically the only exception is the third-person singular pronoun. That is why an English speaker may ask when hearing of a new arrival in a family, "Is it a he or she?" By the way, it is no accident that gender distinction survived among pronouns. A pronoun is a function word; it must refer exactly to

---

93. Снилась is a reflexive form, similar to "to get dressed" in English.

whatever it replaces. I think that is why in English the vestige of declension still exists for this particular word class (e.g., *he/him* and *she/her*).

As a matter of fact, it is not the differences in grammar, vocabulary, and phonetics between languages that we should be surprised at; it is the common features. Without academic ambitions, let me confine myself to the observations of a linguaphile. It is remarkable how many languages used to use the same word to express the activity of winning a lady's heart.

A Hungarian lad used to court somebody (*udvarol*, cf. *udvar* courtyard). To court in German is *den Hof machen*; in French, *faire la cour*; in Italian, *corteggiare*; in Spanish, *hacer la corte*. All reflect court in English.

Even the Russian term ухаживать [ukhazhivat', lit. walk around] suggests that the suitor didn't venture beyond the courtyard. (Actually, this verb has a dual meaning. At the very beginning of my Russian studies I was deeply moved when an aquaintance, Ivan Ivanovich, canceled an invitation because he wanted to ухаживать his sick, old wife. "That's marital fidelity indeed!" I cried out with admiration. My romantic notion lasted until I found out that the word means not only courting but also looking after someone.)

As opposed to court, which is in the international vocabulary, the noun *kert* (yard or garden) gave rise to the verb *kertelni* which is to beat around the bush in English, *aller par quatre chemins* (go by four ways) in French, and *tergiversar* (turn your back [towards the goal]) in Spanish.

I have one more—I promise, my last—argument for reading-based learning. Languages change; these changes sometimes occur as a result of a stroke of a pen, sometimes as a result of a slower process. For instance, "whose" used to apply only to a person (of whom); now it is happily used in reference to objects as well (of which).

You can follow such changes only with the help of books

I make an exception, of course, for the atypical case where you can spend prolonged time in the target country every four or five years and have a partner there who is intelligent, patient, and free to hang out with you. However, it is normally only through literature that you can get acquainted with new expressions and break with old ones.

I recently talked with someone who had gone to school in Paris. Needless to say, his[94] French had a much more solid foundation than my knowledge scraped together in Hungary. Nevertheless, I instantly listed 10 verbs that he didn't know. They had been coined after he had left Paris. But these words had found their way to Hungary via the most recent literature.

It might be in French that vocabulary changes the most rapidly. Ironically enough, nowhere do they guard the purity of the language with such solicitude as in France. Despite all efforts by the officials, French slang, barely comprehensible to foreigners, lives and flourishes.

The control and regulation of the language began with Richelieu and the founding of the *Académie française* in 1634. Since that time, the formal language still wears—as described by Jean-Louis Bory—"lace collar and patent leather shoes."

In the last couple of years, language cultivation has become a pastime in Hungary as well. According to some, it is excessive.

---

94. The gender is unknown from the original Hungarian text.

("In this country there are more people who cultivate the language than the land," I once heard.) In France, however, elaborating the taboos, prohibitions, and commands of the language is the duty of the authorities.

The French Academy, the Ministry of Culture, and the French Language Institute spent more than a year discussing the essential word *cure-pipe* (pipe cleaner). They couldn't decide whether the singular or the plural of pipe is more suitable to the spirit of the language. The October 16, 1981 session of the International Council for the French Language finally decided on the plural.[95]

Various institutions have made serious demands for restoring the past glory of the French language. Apart from patriotism, evidently there are also prestige considerations that play a role in why delegates at international meetings are willing to speak—and even understand—only French. Trade policy interests are not to be neglected, either. France doesn't mean only "the songful fields of Provence"[96] but also the Concorde and excellent computers intended for export.

I am not sure how much it advances the export opportunities of the French that they use special self-made terms instead of the international terminology of information technology. The French use *logiciel* instead of software, even though the latter is widespread throughout the world, *tomodensitomètre* instead of scanner (in computer tomography), and so on.

A 1973 regulation prohibited the use of "marketing" and ordered *mercatique* and *marchéage* to be introduced. Our ancestors

---

95. According to the *Rectifications orthographiques du français en 1990*, the correct form is currently *cure-pipe* in the singular and *cure-pipes* in the plural. The rule applies to the spelling of other compounds of the same type as well.
96. Reference to the poem *Búcsú* ("Farewell") by József Eötvös (1813–1871).

didn't fight with a greater zeal during the Hungarian Reform Era against German borrowings than the French do today against the influx of English into their language, which produces what they call *franglais*.

In France, 66% of scholarly articles are published in English. *Navigare necesse est*—To sail is necessary—it has been proclaimed. French people who want to succeed shrug at the ambitions of the authorities to enforce linguistic prescriptions. *"Publicare necesse est*—in English," they say (It is necessary to publish in English).

The situation is similar in Switzerland. It has four official languages—French, German, Italian, and Romansh—but a fifth is used in academic journals and at conferences—English.

The lack of success of the collective endeavor is obvious by the fact that the French press is laden with terms coined from English: *striptiseuse, speakerine* (a female speaker). At a holiday resort in Provence, the most elegant restaurant is advertised with a neon sign: *Le Kitchen*. Inside, those in a hurry will drive away their hunger with hamburgers and pizzas that can be grabbed quickly, just as in America. Nevertheless, nationalism converted "fast food" to the French-style *fastefoude*.[97]

We should reflect a bit on the factors that brought about the rapid spread of English in the decades following World War II. Disregarding economic and political reasons, let me contemplate the question purely from the point of view of a linguaphile.

Neither Brits nor Americans are inclined to learn other languages. The *Financial Times* (March 19, 1983) describes a linguistic schizophrenia: Despite the UK's ever-increasing export efforts,

---

97. Use of *fastefoude* is negligible today. *Fast-food* might be retained with a hyphen, or synonyms such as *casse-croûte, prêt-à-manger, restoration rapide*, etc. may instead apply to the institution or the food itself.

in the previous year only 138 people in the entire UK applied for the advanced-level language examination.

The English have bad memories of language teaching in schools: Until recently, French and German were taught as Latin had been taught, apparently without much success. I once heard an English tourist at Calais try in vain to understand the speech of a French porter: "I don't know if ships are truly lost at sea in the Bermuda Triangle. But La Manche [the English Channel] absorbs my French skills between Dover and Calais, that is for sure!" he grumbled in fury.

The linguistic and geographic illiteracy of some inhabitants of the US is downright shocking. This sentence appeared in the *Indianapolis Star:* "Switzerland is a country with three [sic] languages which causes [sic] big troubles. For example, the same city [sic] is called *Luzern* in German, *Lausanne* in French, and *Lugano* in Italian."[98]

In multilingual America, higher education is perfectly monolingual. At a teachers' conference in 1979, President Carter lashed out at this system, which he called "the policy of short-sightedness." He proudly stated that he was a rare exception among Americans in that he understood Spanish.

It is a pity he didn't speak Polish. He could have avoided an embarrassing experience that happened to him and which was widely reported in the press. I am ashamed for my profession to cite how an unknown colleague of mine—hitherto an official interpreter for the White House—distorted a sentence of the presi-

---

98. (The exact original sentence cannot be retrieved.) Luzern is in the center and is called *Lucerne* in French and *Lucerna* in Italian. Lausanne is in the west and is called the same in German and *Losanna* in Italian. Lugano is in the south and has the same name in German and French.

dent's 1977 speech in Poland from "I have come to learn your opinions and understand your desires for the future" to "The president desires the Poles carnally."

By the way, at the aforementioned teachers' conference, a decision was made: A new committee would study the issue. Problems may be individual, but proposals for solutions are the same irrespective of continents. The committee came into being, and it continued under the aegis of President Reagan.

21

~

AFTER ALL THIS GOSSIPING about North America, let's have a look around our own house a bit. How do we Hungarians fare in terms of foreign-language skills, with a mother tongue that is sweet for us but doesn't really help us unlock other languages?

The most recent statistics I can rely on are from 1981.[99] Tamás Terestyéni, who compiled them, made surveys in 99 settlements, many inhabited by national minorities (such as Slovaks and Romanians).

The data were provided by the respondents themselves. Even the researcher who compiled the statistics emphasized the danger of subjectivity arising from self-assessment.

The most important finding is that 14.8% of the population of Hungary speaks at least one foreign language. Nearly 6% of the population are ethnic groups who have a non-Hungarian native tongue. The population of non-Hungarian native speakers varies by region. Such speakers are 7.7% of the population in Hajdú-Bihar county and 20.3% in Baranya, which lies by the Yugoslavian border and has always had a mixed population.

I quote the following—also not surprising—excerpt from a collection published in 1980.

---

99. According to the 2012 Eurobarometer survey, 35% of Hungarians reported that they speak at least one foreign language, and 13% at least two. (Source: http://ec.europa.eu/public_opinion/archives/ebs/ebs_386_en.pdf)

Residents who have foreign language skills

Between the ages of 30 and 39	15.2%
Between the ages of 40 and 49	10.2%
Between the ages of 50 and 59	16.8%

What explains the relatively significant decrease in the middle row? Answer: this generation took language classes from 1942 to 1952. Because of World War II, public education was at a crawl, and then post-1948 politics restricted foreign language teaching. In these years, a decree advised children to give up extracurricular language instruction.

Apart from seniors who still speak foreign languages, today we can see many youngsters who already speak them. Young doctors, engineers, economists, lawyers, sociologists, etc. usually understand texts read or heard. They are capable, to a degree, of a conversation in their own field.

However, we cannot be satisfied with the language skills of blue-collar workers. It is especially regrettable in the case of women and men who communicate with foreigners at work. It is an unsolved but important and exciting task to develop a language instruction program for drivers, police officers, conductors, hair stylists, and shop assistants—anyone working downtown or in tourist areas.

One piece of data in the statistics is especially painful. Completion of the eight grades of elementary school raised the percentage of those acquiring language skills by only 0.2% (from 7.0% to 7.2%). The researcher who compiled and evaluated the statistics noted that these graduates received Russian instruction for at least four years. The prediction of future knowledge is even more dismal: Given the current effectiveness of elementary school language teaching, we cannot expect much better results from primary, high-school, or college education.

Many regretful or exhorting articles have been published in connection with this problem. In my book *Polyglot: How I Learn Languages*, I suggested ways to successfully learn languages. Let me now approach the question from the opposite side:

What you should *not* do if you aim to achieve an acceptable level of linguistic mastery within an acceptable time frame

1. *Do not postpone* embarking on learning a new language—or restarting such a study—until the time of a trip abroad. Rather, try to gain access to native speakers who are on a visit to your country and who do not speak your language. They could be relatives or friends. If you accompany them and show them around, out of gratitude they will help you solidify your knowledge of their language; they will enrich your vocabulary and excuse the mistakes you make.

2. *Do not expect* the same behavior from your compatriots. Do not practice with them; they will be prone to giving prime time to your errors—or at the very least, they will be inclined to employ meaningful facial gestures—to demonstrate how much better they are at the language than you.

3. *Do not believe* that a teacher's instruction, no matter how intense and in-depth it may be, gives you an excuse not to delve into the language on your own. For this reason you should, from the outset, start browsing illustrated magazines, listening to radio programs and prerecorded cassettes, watching movies, etc.

4. In your browsing, *do not get obsessed* with words you don't know or structures you don't understand. Build comprehension

on what you already know. Do not automatically reach for the dictionary If you encounter a word or two you don't recognize. If the expression is important, it will reappear and explain itself; if it is not so important, it is no big loss to gloss over it.

5. *Do not skip* writing down your thoughts in the foreign language. Write in simple sentences. For foreign words you can't think of, use one from your own language for the time being.

6. *Do not be deterred* from speaking by a fear of making mistakes. The flow of speech creates a chain reaction: the context will lead you to the correct forms.

7. *Do not forget* to learn a large number of filler expressions and sentence-launching phrases. It is great when you can break the ice with a few formulas that can help you over the initial embarrassment of beginning a conversation, for example, "My French is kind of shaky" or "It's been a while since I spoke Russian," etc.

8. *Do not memorize* any linguistic element (expression) outside of its context, partly because a word may have several meanings. For example, "comforter" may refer to someone who is consoling another, or it can mean a knitted shawl, a quilt or eiderdown, or a baby's pacifier. In addition, it is good, right off the bat, to get used to the practice of abandoning the vortex of meanings around the word in your own language and reaching out to its kin words in the new language (or to the context you have most frequently encountered it in).

9. *Do not leave* newly learned structures or expressions hanging in the air. Fix them in your memory by fitting them into new settings: into your sphere of interest, into the reality of your own life.

10. *Do not be shy* of learning poems or songs by heart. Good diction is more than the mere articulation of individual sounds. Verses and melodies impose constraints; they set which sounds must be long and which must be short. The rhythm helps the learner avoid the intonation traps of his or her native language.

22

~

AS FAR AS I REMEMBER, we were in the United States when we took this long detour. Let's return there now and examine the other reasons for the monolingualism of the US.

Among other things, immigrants to the US endeavor to adapt themselves to American norms as fast as possible; they strive to conform. The second generation is ashamed of their parents' strong foreign accent. "Don't speak Tarzan," I heard a teenager on a New York street growl at his father.

Another reason for American monolingualism is that although American soldiers have fought on other continents, no foreign army has entered the US since 1814, and even then the invaders spoke English.

Let's compare the situation of the US with that of Alsace-Lorraine, where the citizenship and official language changed four times in less than a hundred years. Under Napoleon III, who reigned from 1852–1870, the region's official language was French; after the Battle of Sedan (1870) it was German; following World War I, it was French again. Alsace-Lorraine was German during the five-year Nazi occupation, but French again in 1944. Authorities in the region show great tolerance in matters of language; mother tongue is a generational issue there. Whatever interests youth—sports news, for example—is published only in French in otherwise bilingual newspapers.

English speakers never learned the language of the people they colonized and, out of laziness, tolerated the subjugated people's poor English. Therefore we interpreters are apprehensive at conferences if a Nigerian or a Ghanaian rises to speak. The French, on the other hand, are extremely intolerant of crimes committed against their beautiful language by other nationalities. The French authorities eradicated distortions of French, *petit nègre*, with uncompromising rigor. Therefore, sons and daughters of Algeria, Tunisia, and Vietnam do very well at international meetings. They rarely speak other foreign languages, however. This explains the strange situation of French needing to be included among the languages of a conference exclusively for the sake of colonials once oppressed. There are 100 million German speakers, but Germany has no lost colonies whose inhabitants maintain the prestige of their language in this paradoxical way.

Another reason for the popularity of English is its ostensible ease for learners. Especially at the outset, it lends wings to students, who feel they can make sentences without complicated agreements, by adding word to word. The main bogeyman for learners is English's sequence of tenses, but learners can still speak competent English (even though their utterances may not score highly on language exams). This ease is, however, only ostensible.

There are relatively few chess pieces on the board of today's English. The simplification of the vocabulary and the shortening of words is not new. The Gettysburg Address (1863) was denounced by the *Times* of London as "dull and commonplace."[100] Of its 366 words, 190 are monosyllabic. The address contains no more than 20 two-syllable words.

Long words have been increasingly replaced by short and common ones. Whoever dares to use polysyllables, "dictionary

---

100. In fact the paper used those words to criticize not Lincoln's Gettysburg Address but Edward Everett's.

words," will be stigmatized as a pompous conservative or an egg-head. I would like to show how "dictionary verbs" have been in-creasingly replaced by phrasal (spoken) verbs.

Dictionary verbs	*Phrasal (spoken) verbs*
To endure	To put up with
To extinguish	To put out
To connect	To put through
To invest	To put in
To store	To put away
To repress	To put down
To postpone	To put off
To accommodate	To put up
To reserve	To put aside
To continue	To go on
To enjoy	To go in for
To oppose	To go against
To overtake	To go ahead
To exceed	To go beyond
To mediate	To go between
To escape	To get away
To board (a train, a bus)	To get on
To exit (a train, a bus)	To get off
To rise	To get up
To be accepted by (a school)	To get in
To advance	To get ahead

English has a propensity to shear off the ends of polysyllabic words. This is how perambulator has become *pram*, refrigera-tor *fridge*, magazine *mag*, permanent (wave) *perm*, influenza *flu*, mackintosh *mac*, brassière *bra*, advertisement *ad*, and so on.

The pursuit of brevity begets such oddities as this one, which I recently encountered in a headline:

QE2 in WW2

First I thought it was about some chemical process, but I was wrong: the article gave an account of how bravely Queen Elizabeth II (QE2)—a young woman then—acted in World War II.

French argot has an obsession with similar abbreviations. Whoever stays away from a *manif* (*manifestation*, demonstration) will be soon branded a *réac* (*réactionnaire*, reactionary).

Today's English favors three-letter words. Their structure is almost invariably the same: consonant—vowel—consonant.

During hours of boredom, it may be fun to see how many "smart" squares you can construct—say, within two minutes— where all sides are made up of existing English words:

P	A	D
O		A
T	U	B

R	O	W
U		A
G	A	Y

S	I	T
O		O
N	A	P

and so on.

I have become an expert on the issue, not as a linguaphile but as a passionate Rubik's Cube player

Because I am hooked on languages, I applied for a patent on a cube that has to be turned not until the same colors meet but until meaningful English words—nouns and verbs—are formed.

The patent was declined. As a way of comforting myself, let me insert here the possibilities that I needed for a cube. This is all I found in the English language.

D	I	P
O	R	E
G	E	T

P	I	P
A	C	E
L	E	G

F	I	B
E	V	E
E	Y	E

T	O	N
A	W	E
B	E	T

B	E	D
A	G	E
R	O	W

R	A	P
O	D	E
T	O	P

I tried with other languages and failed. I found only three solutions in Hungarian that comply with the above restrictions:[101]

S	I	P
A	P	A
V	A	D

H	I	T
I	G	A
M	E	R

B	A	B
Ó	R	A
R	A	K

I invite submissions for new combinations, of different words, in any language. First and second prize: a Rubik's Cube. Third prize: a signed copy of this book. Rules: Only nouns and verbs can be used; a word can occur only once in a set. No names, suffixed forms, or abbreviations. No other tricky constructions, please!

---

101. *Síp* whistle; *apa* father; *vad* wild; *sav* acid; *ipa* father-in-law; *pad* bench. *Hit* faith; *iga* yoke; *mer* dare; *hím* male; *ige* verb; *tar* bald-headed. *Bab* bean; *óra* hour/clock; *rak* put; *bór* boron; *ara* fiancée; *bak* buck. A lack of distinction between "i" and the accented "í" is usually allowed in Hungarian crossword puzzles.

23

~

THE BREVITY OF ENGLISH WORDS shouldn't delude anyone into believing that English is easy to learn. It has built-in difficulties; they are built in so cleverly that it takes a fairly long time to notice them. To repeat an old joke: Only the first 10 years are easy; then it becomes more and more difficult.

However, language learners will bump into the first problem at the beginning. The difference between written and pronounced forms is such a big pitfall that it is worth quoting the witty thoughts of a hardened linguaphile and, incidentally, an excellent Spanish writer, Luca de Tena—even if he sometimes goes over the top for the sake of a punchline. Mr. de Tena wrote the following anecdote about English in 1969.[102]

> When I was traveling in the Middle East or in Spain, I found that I could speak English with Egyptians, Jordanians, Syrians, Greeks, and Spaniards—but not with the English.
> The problem is vowels.
> The Latin alphabet has only five. However, these five don't exhaust all the possibilities that a human throat can produce.
> The problem began with the French. Just as you can make green by combining yellow and blue, the French blended the "u" with "i" and gave birth to their special "ü" sound. Their silent "e"— if you'll pardon me—sounds exactly like a discreet belch.
> The English went much further. William Shakespeare's sublime

---

102. "*Las vocales inglesas y las laringitis peninsulares.*" ABC, January 4, 1969.

language uses 18 vowels.[103]

This language would be much easier to learn if the English had devised special signs to mark these special sounds (as the Spanish did with the ñ used on the peninsula). But the English didn't: To describe these 18 noises orthographically, they use those five vowels in the Latin alphabet.

The situation is aggravated by not having rules to prescribe which one to apply in which case. No! Pronunciation is based on traditions, as is the British Constitution, which was never recorded in writing.

The Spanish have a few sounds unsuitable for export as well. For example, "j." Its pronunciation most resembles, of the sounds that humans can produce, the ferocious growl of a lion. The Iberian "j," too, is a superfluous remnant from an age when our ancestors had tails, tore raw flesh to shreds, and climbed trees with their toes (at that time still suitable for grasping). This sound induces lots of troubles—for example, it causes a high rate of laryngitis among the Spanish as well as foreigners who try to pronounce the harsh language of Cervantes in its original form.

Furthermore, there is the double "ll," nicknamed "elle." To approximate the right pronunciation, the tongue needs to do acrobatic stunts. The Republic of Argentina declared independence from this sound sooner than from the Kingdom of Spain. Argentines converted it to a sound more humane and more tolerable: it resembles the smooth braking of a bicycle tire on wet asphalt.

But how does it relate to the 18 vowels in English, whose pronunciation I compare to the warble of the nightingale?

Can you imitate a songbird? If you cannot, you will never speak like the English. And because we don't speak "bird," I am grateful to the Greeks, Egyptians, Syrians, and Jordanians. Thanks to their reduced scale of sounds, I could match the English I read in books with the one they speak.

---

103. The number may vary depending on the dialect and the phonological description.

I cannot say the same for Sir Laurence Olivier and the BBC announcers, whose linguistic preciosity almost made me give up on this language once and for all.

24

~

IT MIGHT BE DUE to the great variety of English sounds that English reveals social class in Britain more noticeably than other European languages reveal class in their countries. Cockney English, common to working-class areas in London, is different from the one spoken by the Upper Class (for short, U).

U English opens doors, procures jobs, and leads to promotions

Our Hungarian nation of 11 million[104] speaks a language that has few dialects. That is why it is difficult for us to grasp that a sharp-eared person can distinguish several levels within U English.

In America, the most prestigious pronunciation can be acquired at an Ivy League university. The walls of the buildings are densely covered by ivy, proof of their several centuries of existence. The less privileged are left with state or, in the UK, redbrick colleges and pronunciation.[105]

We Hungarians will hardly be mistaken for members of any of the above categories. Pronunciation immediately betrays non-natives, even in languages that have less complex phonetic systems. That said, we deserve forbearance when we face sentences in English that are so twisted that they make the logic of our Hungarian language recoil. I picked a bouquet of them out of a contemporary British novel. They have features of English likely

---

104. In 2016, 9.9 million people. Approximately 3 million people speak Hungarian outside the country.
105. Pronunciation differences among US institutions are seldom noticeable.

to be peculiar to Hungarian speakers:

"We all expect you not to mind being stood up by her."
(*Mindannyian reméljük, hogy nem törődsz azzal, hogy cserben hagyott.*—Lit. We all hope that you don't care about it that she failed you.)[106]

"She felt the desire to talk mastering her." (*Érezte, hogy erőt vesz rajta a közlés vágya.*—Lit. She felt that the desire of talking overcame her.)[107]

"One could not think that somebody would have thought of it." (*Nem hinné az ember, hogy valaki gondolt volna erre.*—Lit. The person wouldn't believe that someone would have thought of this.)[108]

"He was hung up on." (*Letették a kagylót, miközben beszélt.*—Lit. They put down the receiver while he was talking.)[109]

"All this should have been seen to by now." (*Mindezzel már eddig is törődni kellett volna.*—Lit. [It] would have been necessary

---

106. "You" seems to be the object of "expect," even though it is not only you that we expect. Equivalents of the infinitive "not to mind" and the gerund "being stood up" are not applicable in Hungarian; full clauses are required for both. The regular passive form is almost non-existent in Hungarian; a conversion to the third person singular is necessary. "Stand sb up" cannot be understood by its elements.

107. "The desire to talk" will become "the desire of talking." The other part of the object is the act of mastering, expressed with a participle (which needs a full clause in Hungarian), separated from "desire." "Master" is used as a verb here and it takes on a special meaning.

108. "One" is expressed in Hungarian as "the person." "Would have thought" is an analytic structure as opposed to the partly synthetic *gondolt volna.*

109. The passive construction needs to be transformed, so the unidentified agent needs to be made explicit into a third-person plural form. "Hang up on sb" cannot be understood by its elements, so it needs to be expounded, making the speaker and the receiver explicit.

to care about all this by now.)[110]

"She is easy to look at and difficult to say no to." (*Jó ránézni és nehéz neki nemet mondani.*—Lit. [It is] good to look at her, and [it is] difficult to say no to her.)[111]

---

110. In Hungarian, "should" requires an impersonal verb, as with "it is necessary." The subject of the original passive sentence needs to be converted into the object of the main verb, which is actually an indirect object in this case. "See to sth" cannot be understood by its elements.

111. The object of a subordinate clause cannot be elevated to become the subject of a main clause in Hungarian.

25

~

IT IS OFTEN SAID that languages are neither logical nor illogical, but a-logical.[112] I don't completely understand this subtle distinction, but I am a bit averse to the fact that "you must go" means "you are *forced* to go," whereas "you must not go" conveys that "you are not *allowed* to go."

"*Few* have the chance" means that not many people have the chance, but "*quite a few* have the chance" implies that many people have the chance. You can form an adverb from an adjective, according to the rules of grammar, by adding the "-ly" suffix, e.g., *slow* and *slowly*. However, in the case of "low," which rhymes with "slow," things are practically reversed. *Lowly* is an adjective (as in "a lowly nature"), but *low* can be an adverb (as in "lie low").

The richness of English vocabulary is sometimes perplexing. I have always been proud of how many synonyms Hungarian has for *fösvény* (miser): *fukar, kicsinyes, szükmarkú,* etc. In English, however, one has to choose from at least 13 variants: stingy, miserly, chintzy, penny-pinching, mean, skinflint, cheap, skimpy, avaricious, niggardly, closefisted, cheeseparing, tightwad…

Nevertheless, the difficulties of English are but an entertaining crossword puzzle compared to the intricacies of Japanese

In British English, the pronunciation of words differs according to social class, and pronunciation generally does not vary

---

112. Strictly speaking, *illogical* means "opposite to logic" and *alogical,* "without logic." In practice, however, the distinction is not always obvious.

when speakers speak to those outside their class. In Japanese, pro-nunciation, vocabulary, and even grammar changes if one speaks to someone outside of his or her class. Speakers will humble them-selves linguistically to minimize the hierarchy of Japanese society.

This is why you can't get a clear answer even to such a simple question as, "How do you say 'to come' in Japanese?" If a guest comes, you use the verb *irassharu* (respectful form); if a friend, *kuru* (simple form). You need to conjugate the verb differently depending on your relationship with the conversation partner.

Japanese sentences are thick with auxiliaries. However, they don't suggest the modality or tense of an action, as in other lan-guages. In fact, they serve to signal the relationship between the conversation partners.

When on the telephone, speakers withdraw into modesty so much that they don't say hello but *moshi moshi*, a humble sort of speaking. As long as the other party is talking, you are supposed to indicate with constant humming that you are present and all ears. Althought it is bad manners in other countries to interrupt the speaker, the Japanese expect incessant interjections: *Naruhodo* (indeed) or *sō desu ne* (that's so). This is how a partner shows in-tense interest in what the speaker says.

Whether a student can ask for a glass of water in a new lan-guage is a criterion for success in learning. For the sake of those preparing for a trip to Japan, I will say here that the way to say it is, *Mizu-o sukoshi kudasai* (Descend to me with some water). In most cases you don't even need to say that. An attentive waiter will ask, *O-mizu-o sashiagemasho-ka?* (May I ascend to you with the water?).

At a Hungarian exhibition in Tokyo, we held a reception

which was graced with the presence of a member of the imperial family. We had already lined up to bow in a row before the distinguished guest, but it turned out that for such occasions, the protocol prescribes a longer greeting. The organizer had to give an impromptu speech, and I had to translate it into Japanese. As that was my first encounter with an earthly descendant of the *Tenno* (Son of Heaven), I had no idea how to linguistically address her imperial majesty. I will be forever grateful to the Japanese man standing next to me. From my terrified facial expression he guessed my problem and quickly whispered the correct conjugation into my ear.

Japanese vocabulary and grammar highlight social differences. And while Japanese culture despises self-assertion and self-demonstration among all people generally, it does so even more for women, for it expects them to use forms that express modesty and indecision.

Women are virtually obliged to finish every sentence with *ka shira* (I wonder). Unless it concerns herself or her own property, she is supposed to insert a special prefix (o-) before words, even if she speaks to her newborn baby. It sounds comical to our ears that a diaper is *o-shime* and a potty is *o-maru*—things to wet or pee into.

I heard the following typical story from a businessman who lives in West Germany. He met a woman from Nikkō, fell in love with her, married her, and learned Japanese excellently from her. A few years later he was scheduled to go to Japan on business. Before going, he contacted his negotiating partners by phone. When he arrived in Japan, they received him with a sigh of relief: So he's still a man, after all! They couldn't reconcile the deep baritone they had heard over the phone with the feminine Japanese phrasing he had used (acquired from his wife).

This anecdote will serve as a segue to my next topic.[113]

The problem of women's language vs. men's language

There is already considerable literature on this issue; one of the most outstanding experts on it is the linguist and translator György Kassai in Paris.

They say that women are more loose-tongued. I read in books on archeology that women's skeletons are characterized as much by their more delicate, more finely chiseled jaws as by their broader hip bones. It is a fact that generally women everywhere speak faster than men do. (According to Mario Pei, the average American male utters 150 syllables per minute, while the average American female utters 175.) Countless jokes, clichés, and comedy routines have been based on the fact that women talk more. This "verbal inflation" is expressed in different ways in different languages, depending on a woman's age and social status.

In English, for example, a little girl "prattles." By the time she gets to school, she "chatters" or "jabbers"; when she grows up she "babbles." A lady "chats," a female colleague "yakety-yaks" or perhaps "blabs," a neighbor "gabs," a bride "twitters," a wife "blathers," a mother-in-law "cackles." A girl-buddy is reprimanded and told to cut the "chinfest." And so on.

Let me interject here, in connection with tongues, what I think accounts for the cliché *Ein Mann ist ein Wort; eine Frau ist ein Wörterbuch* (A man is a word; a woman is a dictionary).

Prehistoric man's meals came from killing prehistoric buffalo. Owing to the stronger male physique, it was natural that men

---

113. The rest of this chapter (translation: Kornelia DeKorne) appears in slightly different form in *Polyglot: How I Learn Languages*.

would go hunting while women stayed at home. Moreover, pregnancy and nursing filled a woman's life; she would not survive her fertile years by much. This was slow to change; even at the turn of the 20th century, the average life expectancy of a woman was only 50 years.

Today we are aware that the brain is compartmentalized: there exists a particular division of labor between the two hemispheres. The right brain governs motion while the left brain plays the decisive role in governing speech and verbal activity.

It is no wonder that in women the right brain has regressed—if not in volume, at least in function—because women move less. At the same time, the left brain, responsible for verbalization/vocalization, has grown in importance. Seventy-five percent of all interpreters, worldwide, are women.

The ideogrammatic part of the Japanese character set reflects the meanings of words. The "hieroglyph" for "man" is 人 because a man walks on two legs and feet and emerges from the animal kingdom with a straight torso. The symbol for "woman," by contrast, is 女—a woman sits and doesn't walk.

As a result of the decreased need and opportunity for moving about, women's capacity for spatial orientation has regressed. In keeping with this, the radius of their sphere of interest has also gotten smaller. It has focused on their immediate environment: people. Let us think of a camera: one narrows its aperture when focusing on nearby objects rather than faraway landscapes.

As a result of this shortening of perspective, women follow personal relationships more closely, recognize their patterns more readily, and talk about them more frequently.

Women have a closer relationship to words. It is therefore logical that the number of women authors is on the rise. It is also interesting to note that their importance is increasing, especially in fiction. Although emotions are well expressed by poetry, poetry requires more pithy, concise forms. With all due apologies to our excellent Hungarian women poets, women's greater affinity with words can flower in the more loquacious genre of prose. I am proud to cite Endre Bajomi Lázár's report on the 1982 French book market: Among authors, the ratio of women to men is 2:1.

It is easy to explain why it was only in the 20th century that women began to dominate fiction writing even though they have always out-talked men. Writing was an unbecoming profession for a lady of rank, even in Jane Austen's time. Austen always kept a muslin scarf handy. Whenever someone approached, she casually tossed it over her manuscript.

Women not only talk more than men, but they also speak differently. It would not be in keeping with the spirit of my book to enumerate here all the experiences eminent researchers have acquired by working in well-known languages (such as French or Russian), as well as in lesser-known ones (Darkhat, Chukchi, or Koasati). I would just say here that, in general, women's speech tends to be protracted, drawn-out. One reason is the doubling of vowels. This style of double emphasis invests words with a strong emotional content.

Men tend to speak more directly. British and American commercials often feature men. Statements such as "Eat this!... Do this!... Buy this!" sound more unequivocal, more absolute.

Members of the social elite have always regarded emphatic, drawn-out speech with disdain and seen it as unmanly, effeminate. Aiming at a reserved, refined demeanor, they have tended toward compact sounds. This is how the French word *beau* (beautiful, handsome) has come to be pronounced approximately like "baw" in order to be regarded as nicely uttered.

Another feature of feminine language is the shift of all con-sonants toward sibilants /ʃ, s, z/ that give a slightly affected tone to speech. I think these phonetic changes play the same role as fashion: to emphasize femininity. The male voice is deeper, due to men's anatomical structure. Today's unisex fashions may not stress gender differences, but I have noticed that young, short-haired women in their uniforms of jeans and T-shirts instinctively start to twitter at a higher pitch when a man appears on the horizon.

Another characteristic of female speech is shifting open vow-els /a, o, u/ toward more closed vowels. This alternation of open and closed vowels has given rise to doublets. For some reason these tend to move from more closed to open across languages: zigzag,[114] teeny-tiny,[115] knickknack, bric-a-brac, fiddle-faddle, mishmash, pitter-patter, Tingeltangel,[116] clopin-clopant,[117] cahin-caha,[118] tittle-tattle, and so on.

Feminine speech is characterized by a heightened emotional emphasis at the syntactic level as well. Women use more adjec-tives, superlatives, and filler expressions such as "well," "of course," "still," "yet," "only," "also," "on the contrary," or "I tell you."

I cannot too strongly recommend learning these so-called dilut-ing agents to students of any language

These are non-negligible negligibles because they provide space to catch one's breath and to recall the more important ele-ments in the sentence.

---

114. The Hungarian equivalent is *cikcakk*.
115. The Hungarian equivalent is *csip-csup*.
116. German: cheap nightclub, honky-tonk.
117. French: limping.
118. French: with difficulty.

My recommendation applies not only to filler words but also to frame expressions. Collect them and use them! There was a time when one heard only women use the expressions "The thing is that..." or "What can I say, I..." Lately, frame expressions have been cropping up in men's discourse, too. Can we perhaps predict that more feminine turns of phrase are going to gain ground with members of the stronger sex? It would not be surprising; the mother tongue, after all, passes from mothers to children.

26

~

MY HOBBY HORSE has run a long way with me; I will have it take me back to my starting point: the Japanese language. It is worth more reflections. If there is a tongue in the world that can truly be understood from the history and geography of the country, Japanese is it. The land area is approximately three times that of Hungary,[119] but Japan has ten times as many people.[120] The population density[121] is further increased by the fact that only a fairly narrow coastal strip is habitable and arable. The inhabitants of this strip are exposed to so much urban noise that, if converted into electricity, it would produce approximately 25,000 kilowatts per day.

A hunting people would have grown aggressive under the influence of such population density. During the time of the development of language, however, the population made its living by farming; that is why personal reserve might have become de rigueur.

Not only the country, but also the language is an island. The mastery of no other language helps unlock it.[122] Linguists claim the same for Hungarian and Basque. The latter was allegedly

---

119. Approximately 146,000 sq. mi.; comparable to the area of Montana.
120. In 1983, approx. 120 million people; i.e., 40% of the population of the US at the time.
121. 822 people per sq. mi., nine times that of the US overall, or approximately that of Massachusetts.
122. A knowledge of Chinese helps students understand some part of written Japanese, but not speech.

learned in five years only by the devil himself, but even he forgot it in five minutes once he didn't need it anymore.

It is the complexity of characters that usually deters even the most hardened linguaphiles from studying Japanese and Chinese. These critics aren't right. Ideograms and pictograms are not the biggest pitfalls of the language. Indeed pictograms reflect the world more directly than alphabets.

Pictograms are simplified pictures. It is worth becoming familiar with some of them.

In Japanese and Chinese, the tree is represented by the image 木, which suggests branches and roots. Two trees next to each other, 林 , are a grove; three, 森 , a forest. We already know that the symbol of man—an animal with a straight torso—is 人. When does man lean against a tree? When he is tired. Therefore, the meaning of the symbol 休 in Japanese is rest or vacation.

It is easy to recognize this sign: 口 a mouth or an orifice, squared for the sake of the brush. A 門 is a gate with two wings. A mouth in a gate 問 means ask or inquire.

凸 and 凹 speak for themselves: they mean convex and concave. The two next to each other mean uneven, bumpy.

Simple connections may explain the successful use of symbols to teach dyslexic children. At a special school for dyslexic students, pupils learned how to identify a sound with an image. By this means they successfully learned the connection between sounds and letters.

The vividness of word images might be an explanation for the low rate of illiteracy in Japan: only 0.1 percent.

27

~

IN LANGUAGES THAT USE ALPHABETS, one can hardly infer meaning from phonetic form. True enough, one will encounter sibilants everywhere in words that mean *s*ipping, *s*upping, *s*niffling, *s*uckling, *s*nuffling. Hungarian: *sz*ürcsöl, *sz*ív, *sz*opik, *sz*ipákol. French: *s*iroter, *s*ucer. Russian: сосать [*s*osat']. German: *sch*nüffeln, *sch*nuppen, *sch*lürfen. I am pleased to report that sniffling (Hungarian *szipákol*) is *shipa-shipa-suru* in Japanese.[123] But you can't play it safe even with onomatopoetic words. The hoarse roosters of foggy Albion (Britain), for instance, don't greet dawn with *kukurikú* (Hungarian) but "cock-a-doodle-doo."

Cats speak a more universal language than their canine counterparts. The English *meow/miaou*, Hungarian *nyávog*, Russian мяукать [myaukat'], German *miauen*, French *miauler*, and Japanese *nya nya naku* sound familiar, but *bark, ugat,* лаять [layat'], *bellen, aboyer,* and *hoeru* do not.

Blabla is not a Hungarian specialty but a frequently used expression in many languages. This, too, is onomatopoeia: *blöken, béget, baa,* etc. mean *bleating.*

The sound "i" generally refers to smaller sizes. Tera (in full: Terézia, cf. Teresa) was *Teri* when she was small; Pista (István, cf. Stephen) was *Pisti*; and András (Andrew) was *Andris*. My favorite is the Spanish *chiquirritín*—it means a tiny tot. On the

---

123. しぱしぱする (shipa shipa suru) more closely refers to blinking (perhaps while sneezing).

other hand, one cannot infer anything from the length or brevity of words. In Hawaii, the tiny little fish hiding in reef crevices is *humuhumunukunukuāpuaʻa*,[124] but its relative the size of a whale is simply *o*.[125]

Unfortunately, we are often deceived by compounds as well. When I first met the French word *saindoux*, I fell into a reverie about its beauty: it means healthy (*sain*) and sweet (*doux*). It must be something beautiful then. What a disappointment it was to learn that it means lard! On the other hand, the combination of *butter* and *fly* may suggest an insect dropped into rancid butter, but together the words mean another creature—for me, the most beautiful.

Returning to Chinese and Japanese, the character that imitates the shape of a swaddled baby (子) means child. We already know the symbol for woman (女). The two together mean good (好). Interestingly, the Japanese pronounce it the same way (*yoi*) that Hungarians do (*jó*, pr. "yo") but the languages have no connection. To avoid accusations of illusory language studies, I don't dare refer to the fact that *só* (salt, pr. "sho") is *shio* in Japanese. In Japanese and Hungarian the possessor precedes the possession (e.g., the gardener's dog). As for names, in Japanese (and in Hungarian, Chinese, and Korean) the first name follows the surname.[126]

Pictorial writing is logical. Let's consider the personal accessory that Russians use against the sun (зонтик, zontik), Italians against water (paracqua), Hungarians and the French against the

---

124. Reef triggerfish, the state fish of Hawaii.
125. The species *o* is unknown. The term for shark (one of the largest living fish) is *manō* in Hawaiian. The whale shark is the largest extant fish species.
126. Vietnamese follows the same convention as well.

rain (esernyő and parapluie), and what the English use for shade (umbrella). The Japanese symbol is obvious and illustrative: 傘.

A further advantage of pictograms is compactness. They have especially great merit in mottos. A recent slogan is "Japanese spirit combined with Western technology." The phrase requires merely four characters; the pronunciation is *Wakon yōsai*. The title of a recent bestseller, *Banshun sōya* (A Troublesome Night in the Late Spring) took me no less than 12 syllables to translate into Hungarian (*A késő tavasz egy zűrös éjszakája*). In this case, too, the original title consists of four characters. They are so beautiful that I can't help writing them here:

$$晚\ 春\ 騷\ 夜$$

Now I would like to share a riddle with my dear readers, albeit not from Japanese but from Chinese. The symbol for a soldier is 兵. His helmeted head, his lance thrust forward, and his two legs can be seen. Its pronunciation is *ping*. But what can possibly be the meaning of the combination below?

$$丘 兵$$

Answer:
(ɓuod ɓuị d)

The difficulty is that a character doesn't reveal much about how to pronounce it. The pronunciation of a character has to be looked up and learned separately from what it means. In the language of computer science, you need to enter one more piece of information into your memory. In addition, every symbol has several pronunciations. The context decides which one.[127]

If you encounter somewhere the sign 入口, you quickly realize that it combines the symbols 入 (enter) and the already known 口 (mouth, orifice); the meaning is entrance. The pronunciation, however, is much more difficult to get right. When it stands separately, 入 is read as *nyū* and 口 is *ko*, yet together they are *iriguchi*.

Nevertheless, the greatest difficulty is the high number of homophonic words (those with the same sound). The phonetic idiosyncrasy of the language is rather large. A syllable cannot end in anything but a vowel or *n*. The language regards consonant clusters as barbaric and refuses to pronounce them; it always inserts a vowel between two consonants. For this reason, even international words—which provide convenient handholds in other languages—don't rush to aid us. *Berugī* is not easy to identify as Belgium, nor is *Buryusseru* for its capital. The favorite drink of Japanese youth is *Pepushikōra* (Pepsi-Cola).

Even with pictograms, you can't always figure out what they represent. The sun 日 and the crescent moon 月 are square rather than round.[128] The dots (in today's script, horizontal lines) in 日 and 月 are believed to outline sun- and moonspots, visible even to the naked eye.[129] The combination of the two (明) means light or clear. It is not a pictogram anymore but an ideogram: it conveys

---

127. It is mostly true of Japanese, whereas predictability is considerably higher in Chinese (up to 80%). For example, in Chinese 媽, 嗎, 螞, 碼, 瑪, 榪, 獁, 傌, 馮, 遇, 鎷, 禡, 瘬, 鄢, and 罵 are all pronounced "ma" (with different tones, though), which can be presumed from the common phonetic component 馬 (ma, horse) in all these above. Such phonetic elements may—although not infallibly—give clues to pronunciation in Chinese.

128. Originally circular, the characters became angular through brushwork.

129. Some scholars believe that the lines illustrate the celestial bodies themselves, with the center lines showing that the bodies are not empty.

an idea, a concept. But it is still more illustrative than the alternatives in other languages.

Every nation considers its own tongue more logical than others'

We Hungarians (Magyars) reckon that if something is unclear, it needs to be *magyarázni* (explained). According to the German (Deutsch) language, interpreting (construing) is *deuten*. If someone gives his opinion to his friend in no uncertain terms (*magyarán*), he—according to the French—"parle *français* a son ami." "¡Habla en *castellano*!" ("Speak Spanish!") one may say impatiently if he feels his partner is equivocating.

Obscurity and incomprehensibility are often imputed to foreign languages. Another term in English for gibberish is "double Dutch," Dutch meaning the language of old Teutonic tribes. For a German, gibberish is "Kauder*welsch*."[130] For Russians and Hungarians, Germans are немец [nemets], *német*—lit. mute. Whoever uses French in a distorted, incorrect way speaks *petit nègre* (in short, *pègre*) according to the Gauls, proud of their language. The meaning of *barbaros* in Greek is stutterer. What we Hungarians don't understand is "Chinese for us," whereas Italians say *parla in latino* (he speaks Latin) about one who speaks unintelligibly on purpose.

Now that we are at chauvinism, it is worth spending a little time on nicknames applied to other peoples.

The French target of derision is the uncouth German student who dwells among beer mugs, the *Bursch*; that's where the demeaning word *boche* comes from. The English mock Germans as

---

130. It is believed that *welsch* originally referred to the Celtic tribe of Volcae in the south of France; later it came to refer to (speakers of) Romance languages, especially French or Italian.

Kraut, as their main dish is cabbage. The English cannot forgive the French for eating frog's legs, hence the sobriquet *frogs*. Instead, the English like large pieces of roast beef. I have seen an English guest staring at my ragout in horror: "What? You eat the legs of the chicken?"

Where does the term *Yankee* come from? According to one version, it comes from the Dutch given name *Yanke,* which was so fashionable in the 18th century that those in America simply stuck it to all those arriving from Europe. Another explanation is that *Yankee* derives from the pronunciation of the English word *English* in one of the languages of the Native Americans. Nevertheless, it is used today to abuse Americans, sometimes in the shortened form *Yank*.[131]

In World War II, English soldiers were nicknamed *Tommies,* American ones, *Sammies,* from the two most widespread first names.

French pedestrians used to march in North African colonies in knee-high black leather boots. That is why their descendants are still named *pieds noirs*, Blackfeet.

The scornful word *dago* was born from the common Spanish name *Diego,* later extended to the Italians and Portuguese as well. According to another theory, the reason for this nickname is that job-seekers filtered into America through the city of San Diego, close to Mexico. But I also heard that it originates from *digo* —"I say"— frequently interspersed in Italians' speech. In any case, *digo* is the source of *digózás* (dealing with Digos)—Hungarian pretty girls making friends with Italian gallants.

Some recent arrivals in America are taunted as *spicks* ("I no

---

131. Residents of the Southern US will sometimes use *Yankee* as a pejorative for Northerners.

speak English"). In Mexico, however, Americans are derided as *gringos*,[132] reportedly from the first words of the former soldiers' song "Green grows the lilac tree..." Ferenc Karinthy writes that Hungarian men in Italy are named *Signori Preghi* as they begin each of their sentences with *prego* (I ask you) rather than *per favore*, which is customary in Italy.

A Soviet acquaintance of mine warned me not to use венгерка [vengerka], which is the feminine form of Hungarian, i.e., a Hungarian woman or girl. The word was once used for women spirited from the nightclubs of Pest-Buda[133] to Moscow, to entertain the officers of the Tsarist army.

English navy doctors used to prescribe the juice of a lemon-like fruit, lime, for scurvy. Sailors had no idea that they would be teased as *limeys* by Americans.

After derogatory names dictated by national chauvinism, let's console ourselves with "good speech": euphemisms. They are also called linguistic fig leaves as they cover whatever must be covered. More exactly, euphemisms cover whatever an era considers vulgar.

We shouldn't think that we pioneered outspokenness. Shakespeare's works were only made permissible for schoolchildren by the intervention of Thomas Bowdler, *ad usum delphini*.[134] Shakespeare's works, in their unbowdlerized forms, describe certain situations more crudely than do some of today's novelists. In the original, Romeo and Juliet's lacy and delicate love is backdropped by ribald men's jokes.

It was necessary in the mid-19th century to expurgate these

132. Today: *gabachos.*
133. The former, now obsolete, name for Budapest.
134. The phrase derives from the fact that books were rewritten and tamed for the heir to the French throne—the dauphin.

masterpieces to make them suitable for the court. After the stern Middle Ages, the Victorian Period was the most hypocriti- cal age. The Queen gave birth to several children, yet she was a typical spinster (the word doesn't sound as contemptuous as the Hungarian *vénkisasszony*, lit. old miss). This is when a legion of expressions became taboo, several of them for religious reasons, including "hell," "damned," and "bloody." A Victorian lady faint- ed if someone uttered "leg" in her presence. "Bloody" is said to be a reference to Christ's blood, and it was once considered so unut- terable that the whole Empire blushed when G. B. Shaw wrote it. It is still occasionally paraphrased as the Shavian adjective.

Victorian overrefinement is still remembered today in a number of linguistic fig leaves

"Heartburn," for instance, doesn't mean the burning of the heart, as one might intuit by its components, but simply "reflux."

"To sleep with a woman" is an obvious fig leaf; in Spanish, *hacer cositas* (do little things) serves the same purpose. In French, *coucher avec une femme* (sleep with a woman) is the acceptable expression of an unacceptable verb (*baiser*). But who understands that *baiser* is completely acceptable as a noun? Rodin gave his most beautiful sculpture the title *Le Baiser* (The Kiss). I thought that the Hungarian verb derived from that too, but I was wrong: It is of Turkish origin.[135]

The fact that this activity can be expressed gently but not less tangibly is exemplified by Dante's description of the fall of Paolo and Francesca da Rimini: *Quel giorno più non vi leggemmo avante.* In Longfellow's translation: That day no farther did we read there-

---

135. *Baszik. Basmak* means "to press" in Turkish.

in.[136]

We don't any longer feel the euphemistic nature of many Hungarian words. *Farkas* (wolf, lit. tailed [one]) and *szarvas* (deer, lit. horned [one]) are, in fact, *circumlocutory* words, as is the Russian медведь, medved'—a "honeyknower," that is, a bear. At the back of the mind there persisted the superstition that one can keep danger at bay by bypassing the name of a taboo or feared reality.

The numerous fig leaves that developed in every language around death are supposed to expel the terror of the greatest and most unavoidable danger. In Hungarian, the phrases "he returned to his ancestors" (*megtért őseihez*), "he had his suffering over" (*kiszenvedett*), "he turned in the key" (*beadta a kulcsot*), "he went to Földvár [Earth Castle, a place name] to sell planks" (*elment Földvárra deszkát árulni*) can be read only in old books, but "deceased" (*elhunyt*[137]) is still a living euphemism. In English, there are a multitude of bashful or crude circumlocutions: "he passed away," "he gave up the ghost," "he kicked the bucket," "he bought the farm," and "he cashed in his chips"—all are untranslatable idioms that have the same meaning.

The English noun "undertaker" (mortician) is quite distinct from the meaning of the verb "to undertake" (to start a task or endeavor). Many Hungarians fleeing from Nazism to England wrote "undertaker" (thinking of the verb form) in the "Occupation" blank of their immigration applications. This caused the British

---

136. Inferno, Canto V. The original Hungarian edition cites the translation by Mihály Babits ("*Aznap többet nem olvasánk azontúl*") and the one by Sándor Weöres ("*Aznap nem olvastunk már egy betűt se*").
137. *Elhuny* formally meant "go out" (of light), as *kihuny* does today. They are related to *behuny* "close" (the eyes), whereas *huny* means "sleep" in folkspeech. *El-* means "away," as does de- in depart and decease.

authorities to rack their brains as to why there were so many morticians in such a small country.

The prudery of every age picks a fig leaf to hide the natural fact of pregnancy (which is nevertheless difficult to conceal). Until the mid-19th century, the accepted English euphemism was, "She cancelled her social engagements." In the early 20th century, it came into vogue to say, "She is in the family way." Twenty or thirty years later the English said, "She is expecting." It was not until more recent times that "pregnant" became sayable and writable.

"Toilette" was formed by Alexander Pope from *toile* (fabric, canvas). It originally meant a cubicle in which ladies hung their clothes. Interestingly, the English word "closet" retains this meaning. "W.C." is not used in England. I learned in London that "in better circles" a hostess is supposed to ask the guest, "Shall I show you the geography of the house?" The circumlocution, "Do you want to spend a penny?" (which originally referred to coin-operated lavatories) was not upper-class anymore. It no longer belonged to the discourse of high society.

The modern age is not bashful. Euphemisms for procreation or metabolism have been replaced by expressions considered unsayable a generation earlier. We use affected roundabouts for one expression, "old age," which once carried prestige.

It is out of the scope of linguistics, but let me mention three reasons for this loss of prestige. The first is our longer lives. When the average lifetime was 50 years, old age had the value of rarity, like an uncommon postage stamp.

The second reason is that with the increase in schooling, the value of directly passing on experience decreased. Long ago, would-be weavers, blacksmiths, painters, and sculptors acquired their knowledge by apprenticing with masters. Today we go to schools and colleges.

The third reason is the rapid obsolescence of knowledge. It expires so speedily that before long what matters will not be who knows what, but who can forget the old and learn the new as fast as possible.

To gloss over old age, which is now devoid of its rank, a host of euphemisms arose. It is called *troisième âge* (third age) in French. The Germans use *Seniorenwelt* (the world of the elderly). American television wouldn't for the world use the phrase "old age"; the obligatory term is "seniors."

Formal addresses remind us that old age at one time meant rank and respect. *Monsieur, Mister, Signore* are—literally—"my old guy." The Chinese *Xiānshēng* and the Japanese *Sensei* mean "born-before-me." I don't know what a Spanish *grande dame* would say if she knew that *Señora* actually means "old girl."

28

~

THE REASON I HARPED SO LONG on the issue of age vs. language is that I am often asked what is the best age to begin learning a foreign language. I am also asked what is the oldest age when one can learn a language.[138]

The first question concerns mainly parents. The second one concerns pensioners looking for a useful pastime.

Let's start with the first question.

I will cite an experiment that involved swimming lessons for babies. The conductors of the experiment observed that babies two weeks old would frolic uninhibited in basins suited to their size. It was theorized that the babies still had in their neurons the memory of the months spent in amniotic fluid. But six months after birth, the babies would not submerge themselves in the water; they had grown used to the phenomenon of air.

This is more or less the case with language. The mother tongue is inhibition and prejudice. I have seen four- or five-year-old children stamping their feet in anger and even threatening with their fists a person who looks human but is incomprehensible.

The usual argument against playful foreign language instruction that begins before prejudices can set in is, "The child won't learn either language very well." To be frank, I have never seen an example of that in my life. If that were the case, the bilingual children raised at the borders and by nannies would be idiots.

---

138. Pages 171–2 appear in slightly different form in *Polyglot: How I Learn Languages*, pp. 51–52.

My objection to early foreign language instruction, especially by relatives, is that it is rarely effective. Yet if one parent is a native speaker of a language foreign to the environment, let him or her make use of the opportunity to teach a still-pliable mind. The child will have the great advantage of learning native-like pronunciation.

Youth is the age of the development of skills in language learning; it is the period of mechanical imitation of foreign sounds

Today we know that neurons play a role in practicing automatisms and developing proficiency in acquiring knowledge. For the former, pyramidal cells are responsible, and for sorting and analyzing knowledge, stellate cells. The development of pyramidal cells lasts for 12–14 years, then stops. The maturing of the stellate cells ends later.

Whoever comes into contact with a foreign language *after* the cessation of growth of the cells responsible for developing skills will not be able to shed the phonetic norms ingrained from one's native tongue even if he or she lives in the target country for half a century.

Late in life I chose languages as my hobby and vocation. I admit I have never been taken for a native speaker in any foreign country. If I complain about it, the most I can get is this consolation: "Why, we find the Hungarian accent lovely."

Nevertheless, I don't accept the view that no one beyond middle age can learn a foreign language. I often hear people voicing this mistaken belief, and when I disabuse them of it, they usually argue that "Sometimes I forget even my neighbor's name," or "I can't even recall the street where I used to live," or "I can't recognize people who say hello to me, even though we go to the swimming pool together every day." But remembering names and faces is not typical.

I cannot avoid a bit of dry philosophizing about language learning and age.

What children do is *perceive.* They comprehend every phenomenon separately, as individual cases; they don't yet know concepts. "What are you going to be when you grow up?", the clever adult's question goes. We often get answers like, "I'd like to be Uncle Steve (or Aunt Helen)." The *category* of driver, car mechanic, kindergarten teacher, or doctor hasn't developed in them yet.

As they grow older, children will gradually discover the common traits of objects and people, and they learn how to group individuals by these group traits. Thus concepts develop in their minds. An adult *categorizes*—an elderly person even more so.

In old age, connections become clearer, outlines of groups more definite. "Things of the world" live in them inside contexts; details within the fabric stick closely together and become a blur. But whatever cannot be classified by logic and has no place in the context will be difficult for the mind to recall. Names and faces are examples.

Logic has nothing to do with either. The name of a former classmate could be Jones or just as well Smith; I can't place a face when I see it out of its context. It is a well-known phenomenon that a grandfather adores his grandchildren but the category "grandchild" lives in his mind between such solid outlines that he has to try five or six names *within* this category before he can find the name of the grandchild standing in front of him.

29

~

WHEVER IS NOT INTERESTED in the problems of "a mature age," please kindly skip a few paragraphs, because I'd like to theorize a bit more on whether there are characteristics of old people's speech.

If there are, then these qualities are probably caused by a large amount of accumulated experience. If someone has lived, seen, and heard enough, everything will remind her or him of something.

And whatever occurs to an old person will usually be repeated, inducing impatience from members of the younger generation.

In English, the age when mental capacities start to decline is called "dotage." The old gentleman telling anecdotes is well-known. As the saying goes, "He is in his *anecdotage*."

By the time people reach this point, their professions, living conditions, family, and work relationships have polished their characters and abilities very differently. They resemble each other much less than young people, whose journeys have been shorter and thus have had less opportunity to differentiate. And young people's language—let's call it, by analogy to Chinese and Japanese, *teenagerese*—has less variation.

What's more, features transcend country borders. This international quality is a fairly new phenomenon and the result of technological achievements. The simplification of transportation and the growth of television, radio, and recorded media have made it possible for the world to stratify horizontally—by generations.

A generation ago, children chose heroes and outstanding fig-
ures from their own homeland. Today, teenagers idolize many of
the same stars—astronauts, athletes, or pop singers—from San
Francisco to Tirana.

If Hungarian, German, and British teens do not have common heroes, at least their language has commonalities that transcend linguistic boundaries.

Why is it that adolescents develop this special tongue?
Because the teenage years are a sandwich age: Biological changes
in their bodies already separate them from children, but they are
not yet accepted into the world of adults. Teens become aggressive
and develop their own language as a weapon of resistance. Their
speech is both a symbol of alliance with their peers and a symbol
of defiance against the elderly. Communication within communication is proof of belonging.

This language leaves grammar intact; at most teens make even
more use of verb suffixes than adults do. They buzz off, crack up,
freak out, dash off, hook up, and conk out.[139] They rarely ever create new word stems; if they do, it is only within their own narrow
sphere of interest: a few synonyms for women and sex acts, fewer
for money, none for disease or death. (In any case, word-coining
imagination works only in domains illuminated by the lightbeam
of one's interest. Among Inuits, as I read in a guidebook, rotten
fishbladder is one of the most desirable delicacies. To describe its
aroma—that is, its degree of rottenness—there are no less than 11
adjectives available.)

When I was young, teenage boys called girls *tyúk* (hen), *pipi*
(chick), *növény* (plant), *csibe* (chicken), and other belittling ex-

---

139. The original Hungarian lists 12 such terms: *elhúz, lekopik, eldzsal, begőzöl,
kiborul, berág, ráharap, bezsong, kiakad, becsajozik, lerohad,* and *eldobja magát.*

pressions to enhance their masculine self-esteem and conceal their shyness. Today, *csaj* has become prevalent. In our unisex world, this word—borrowed from the Romany language—is only used for women. Its rival, *bula*, may be of German descent, deriving from *Buhlerin* (pretty woman).

Our rich adjectives have become bland

"Awesome," "smashing," and "terrific"[140] can be applied at any point on the scale of appreciation. The subtlety of young people's words has faded. *Izé* ("thing," an all-purpose replacement word) has been replaced by *téma* (lit. theme, topic). "What are you looking for?" I asked a teenager the other day who was groping for something on our dark staircase. "That ... that ... switchy stuff," he replied.

Of course, it is possible that by the time these lines see the light of day, *téma* will have dropped out of our vocabulary and will sound as obsolete as *hon* (homeland) or *hitves* (spouse).

According to Alvin Toffler, in the future the line of demarcation will not lie between North and South or black and white, but between young and old. The detachment process causes sometimes greater, sometimes smaller excitement. The greatest one, that of the 1968 Paris student protest, has already subsided. The young people on the barricades have become tamed into fathers and mothers, married with children. They no longer voice the slogan "Don't trust anybody over 30." Their effect is, however, lasting and irreversible.

Just as the Third Estate of the bourgeoisie appeared on the scene after the French Revolution, and the Fourth Estate (work-

---

140. The Hungarian examples in the original are *haláli* (lit. deathly), *oltári* (altarly), *állati* (lit. animal-like).

ers) at the end of the 19th century, so has a so-called Fifth Estate (youth) appeared. Their role is already significant in the consumption of goods; companies pay close attention to trends in their tastes. Advertising experts rack their brains to invent slogans that impress the youth; at elections, candidates strive to conquer the young by advocating progressive programs. The young will increasingly prevail in the development of languages. I hope that their fresh strength will not impoverish our sweet mother tongue but will enrich it with a new level of style.

30

~

LET'S RETURN FROM THE FUTURE to the present and, instead of speaking of levels of style, let's speak about levels of linguistic mastery. It is a schoolish topic, so let us use a basic grading system to assess the competency of learners.[141]

Tourist level. With a handful of sentences, learners at the tourist level can ask for a train ticket and look for a room, order lunch, and inquire when the evening express leaves. They can figure out from the papers what is showing at the movies, and they can try to haggle down the price of shoes a bit.

Conversational level. Those who are at the conversational level can make contacts as a guest or a host, give an account of their country, inquire about their partner's country, and say what they do. They can also understand when their interlocuter responds in kind.[142]

---

141. The rest of this chapter appears in somewhat different form in *Polyglot: How I Learn Languages*, pp. 167–168.

142. Author's note: I interrupt myself here to give some practical advice to those preparing to go to America. On the train, in the hotel lounge, or at the breakfast table, those sitting next to you will ask you the same questions. First question: "Where are you from?" Second: "What do you do?" Third: "What do you drive?" When I was a novice traveler, I admitted that I usually took the bus. People were so astonished that I changed my answer. I now say, "I don't think you know the make—it's an Ikarus." "Is it a big car?" they would ask. "Is it bigger than a Chevrolet?" "Much bigger!" I would reply with a quick flip of the wrist. [Ikarus is a Hungarian bus manufacturer.] I can only hope that the pagan Hermes and the Catholic Saint Christopher, the patron saint of transportation, will forgive me for my fibbing. I truly don't venture to do so for my own sake but for the prestige of my homeland.

EX-IN level (Export-Import level). Whoever reaches this point can fluently converse in his or her field. The field doesn't have to be foreign trade (export-import) but any discipline. The EX-IN student's passive and active vocabulary is 100% within his or her field. These students can express their thoughts in correct grammar and understandable pronunciation. Outside their profession, however, they tend to converse quite uncertainly.

Last summer I attended an important international conference led by a Hungarian engineer. He sold several thousand electrical appliances to a foreign partner without ever having to resort to the international language of drawings and diagrams that specified types and sizes.

During a break, we presented the foreign partner with an ice cream, which he ate with apparent delight. "Does it taste you?" the Hungarian engineer asked in English, faithful to the Hungarian form.[143] The poor guest was so frightened that I wanted to comfort him with the words of a song from a film: "It won't eat you, it'll only taste you."[144]

Interpreting level. At this level one should know a wide range of vocabulary in a wide range of fields, be able to find the key for a variety of pronunciations in an instant, and know how to render messages in the target language as closely as possible to the thought in the source language, in content and style.

Native level. This is the highest level one can achieve. The native level is when our countryman is taken for a native-born

---

143. The Hungarian equivalent is *"Ízlik?"* (Do you like it?)—but its subject is the food, and the person who enjoys it is in the dative case, cf. "Does it please you?" in English.

144. Reference to the Hungarian translation of the song "Who's Afraid of the Big Bad Wolf?" in Walt Disney's short film.

Frenchman, Russian, Brit, etc. In other words, when he or she speaks Hungarian in Paris, Moscow, or London, people will ask in amazement: What is this interesting-sounding language, and who put it in your head to learn it?

31

~

AM I PERHAPS PARTIAL to my profession? Maybe. But even after having practiced it for several decades, I think one is supposed to approach its pitfalls and difficulties with humility.

Interpreting (simultaneous or consecutive) is an absurd activity

Imagine a metal worker who knows only his job: To make a die of a certain size and shape. However, he knows nothing about the raw material from which he must manufacture it, not even whether it will be suitable for forging, rolling, or drawing. He will not know this until the flowing, quickly cooling metal snake arrives near him. It is no wonder then that a simultaneous interpreter's nerves are held in constant tension by the uncertainties of her task, as she often doesn't know the source language from which she must manufacture, in the next moment, ready pieces of sculpture—sound sentences—in the target language.

Interpreting is a schizophrenic activity

While the interpreter's mouth says target-language sentence *A* into the microphone, her ear is already comprehending sentence *B* and sending it to her brain, which translates and forwards the thought. Those affected with schizophrenia have a head start.

Interpreting is an activity laden with compromise

One can only hew one's way through so many pitfalls by constantly making compromises. "That is how I should—this is how I can." Those who would reject *good* for the pursuit of *perfect* should choose a gentler trade for themselves.

Interpreting is a paradoxical activity

It is a dialogue with three parties: the speaker, the listener, and the translator. It is an improvised genre, a special *commedia dell'arte*,[145] in which there are no defined roles (bon vivants, soubrettes, or tragediennes) because the interpreter will go on the stage sometimes as a man, woman, engineer, doctor, musicologist, or politician. But the interpreter should be invisible, so to speak. A literary translation is good if readers believe that they see the original text. Interpreters are at the top of their profession if no one notices that they mediate the communication process.

Apart from conscientious preparation, routine helps us surmount difficulties. Practice teaches interpreters' minds to respond to the source-language word stimulus—more or less automatically—with target-language words. Within this established strategy, we need only to apply watchful and flexible tactics when we face the main enemy of our trade:

False friends (*les faux amis*)

This is the name of words whose sounds are identical or similar but whose meanings differ between languages.

Despite the fact that they occur even in everyday speech, their fraudulent nature can surprise us. To illustrate, I have picked stories others told me or incidents I experienced myself.[146]

---

145. In full: *commedia dell'arte all'improvviso*—"comedy of the very creative ability of improvisation," a genre originating from 16th century Italy.
146. Eleven paragraphs of the following section on false friends appear in slightly different form in *Polyglot: How I Learn Languages*.

Señor Gonzalez wished to spend a weekend in London. He brought with him the addresses of many boarding houses, yet he had to spend the night in a London park. Why? The reason is that although there were signs saying "Vacancy" on the doors of most of the boarding houses, he confused the word with the Spanish word *vacación*, which means "vacation," "shutdown," or "cessation of activity." And so he only knocked on the doors where he didn't see such a notice. He was unfortunately rejected at those places.

It was in Sevilla where Signore Rossi fared badly. Trusting in the similarities between Spanish and Italian, he asked for butter for breakfast by saying *burro*. After some delay, his hotel produced a beautifully harnessed donkey! (what *burro* means in Spanish). [I note in passing that a Hungarian wishing to ride a *szamár* (donkey) from Capri to Anacapri can safely order a *somaro* because that is indeed the correct term.[147]]

False friends have caused even greater trouble. Once a Frenchman submitted a *demande* (request) at a meeting. However, a "demand" means more than a mere request in English; it is an *emphatic* request. The British representative found this immodesty offensive and immediately vetoed it.

One would assume that there are no false friends in the world of mathematics, that numbers do speak an international language. Unfortunately, that is not the case. In most European countries "billion" is 1,000,000 × 1,000,000, a million times a million, expressed as 10^{12}. In the States, however, it is only 1,000 × 1,000,000, a thousand times a million, expressed as 10^9. This figure is called *milliard* in most of Europe.

Titles, ranks, and school types are often unique to a country.

---

147. Capri and Anacapri are townships on the Italian island of Capri. The Hungarian word for donkey is *szamár*.

A Hungarian *akadémikus* (academician, member of the Academy of Sciences) is not the same as a German *Akademiker*. The latter is only someone who has graduated from a university or college. A university or college is *Hochschule* in German, but in America "high school" refers to a secondary school—roughly like *gimnázium* in Hungarian. *Gymnasium*, on the other hand, means a sport facility in English and comes from the Greek *gymnos* (naked).

The Russian word институт [institut] doesn't mean "institute," as in other languages, but it is a common denomination of universities and colleges that provide the highest level of education in medicine, engineering, and agriculture. Whoever graduates from them can continue their studies as an *aspirant* (i.e., longing, cf. PhD student), then as a *candidate* (cf. PhD holder). The apex is "doctor of sciences" (conferred by the Academy of Sciences), which is called "grand doctorate" in Hungary.[148]

A "doctor" is an old, prestigious rank that derives from *doctus* in Latin. In the old times, it applied to anyone who created something excellent in any trade. For instance, the grave of the court architect of the French King Saint Louis (Louis IX) reads that the one resting there was a *Docteur des pierres*—a scholar of stones.

When I learned that the father of my friend in Madrid had had a car accident, I inquired about his health by phone. "*Esperamos su muerte*," I was told. I hung up in shock. It was only later when I realized that the verb *esperar* means "to wait" or "to expect," not just "to hope," as does the French *espérer*.[149] I also learned that someone who *prematuramente jubilado* did not jubilate (rejoice) too soon but retired early. On the other hand, it was

---

148. It was replaced by the international system of PhDs in the 1990s.
149. In other words, Lomb mistook "We expect his death" for "We hope for his death."

a pleasant surprise that the Hungarian *cédula* (note, slip of paper) is also *cédula* in Spanish (document), and a scribe is a *chupatintas* (which in Hungarian recalls someone completely [*csupa*] covered with ink [*tinta*]).

The Hungarian *kokett* was used to mean "coquettish" when I was young. Its French meaning is much more general: e.g., *une somme coquette*—a tidy sum. *Il est coquet pour son âge* means "There's life in the old dog yet."

I am angry with English because "he blames himself" doesn't mean *blamálja magát* (to make a fool of oneself, to disgrace oneself), and I am disappointed with Spanish because *compromiso* is not only a compromise but a commitment or engagement.

The following blunder occurred in a Hungarian-Polish business deal. A cosmetics factory in Warsaw believed it had invented a miraculous anti-wrinkle face cream; it offered its distribution in Hungary to a Hungarian foreign trade company. A rather awkward correspondence took place in French; the Polish client called the agent of the cream *agent à dérider* (*ride:* wrinkle). Her Hungarian partner conscientiously looked up the words in the dictionary and established that *agent* means "a police officer" and *dérider* "detection." Luckily she didn't order a considerable amount for the Hungarian police; she simply replied by mail that "such things are outside the profile of our company."

In the Netherlands one should be careful with the word *monster*. It means "sample." "Attention" is *Aandacht* in Dutch, but *andacht* in German means "devotion." I would have certainly translated the Portuguese word *importância* as "importance" had I not realized from the context that it means "amount."

An Italian beau will not succeed if he flatters a German woman by saying that he finds her *calda* and *morbida* (warm and soft), because *calda* connotes *kalt* (cold) and *morbida* recalls *Morbidität* (morbidity). Neither should a Frenchman praise the beautiful *denture* of his English partner; it means natural teeth in his lan guage but the opposite in English.

As they say, only a kleptomaniac will steal something he doesn't need. Likewise, languages won't normally borrow foreign words unless they lack a term for the underlying concept.[150] Hungarian ladies started to dress in the Viennese fashion in the mid-19th century. They imported *slicc* (placket, fly, cf. *Schlitz*), *másli* (bow, ribbon, cf. *Masche*), and *míder* (bodice, cf. *Mieder*) along with clothes. We borrowed *ukáz* (edict, order) from Tsarist Russia and *szputnyik* from the Soviet Union, *weekend* from English, and *dolce vita* from today's Italy.

The word "Levantine"—a word of Latin origin meaning "Eastern"—is used worldwide to describe a certain human type,[151] but "Ponientine" (or Ponente, lit. a wind from the West) hasn't made its way into international terminology: We presume to dis cover common traits between Easterners, but not Westerners.

Loanwords sometimes impolitely reflect the recipient nation's opinion of the host nation. *Obsequioso* means only "obliging" in Spanish. English speakers, however, apparently finding Spanish gallantry excessive, used *obsequious* in the sense of "fawning." *Obsèques* in French is a funeral rite.[152] The French imported a Spanish word to express "bragging": it took over *jactancia* and created *jactance* out of it.

---

150. Apart from this, other factors, such as perceived elegance or brevity, can account for the spread of new loanwords.

151. People from countries bordering the eastern Mediterranean Sea.

152. *Obsequious* comes from Latin *obsequi* "to comply." *Obsèques* (cf. obsequies in English, the plural of obsequy), on the other hand, derives from *obsequiae*, alteration of Latin *exsequiae*, from *exsequi* "to follow out," "to execute."

From German, *Weltschmerz* (world-weariness) entered the international terminology, but I know that the world doesn't know Germans only from their romantic side. During the Tokyo student protests of the 1960s, I frequently tried to find out from the young people marching in a serpentine way how they thought they could solve their problems. The answer was always the same: *Gebaru.* It took me a while to realize that they had distorted the German *Gewalt* (force) to suit the Japanese tongue.

Work has a central place in the life of every nation and thus its language. It is no accident that even my amateurish comparative vocabulary research can reveal an array of linguistic oddities on this subject.

The Latin word *labor* (work) became the French *labour*, in the meaning of tillage, plowing. A *laboureur* is a husbandman. In English, a *laborer* is an unskilled worker.

The result of work is accomplishment—in Latin, *opus.* Its plural—*opera*—means a vocal performance in every language. In French, opus has become *œuvre*, but a *dame d'œuvre* is a woman who does charity, whereas a *woman in labor* is about to give birth. This reminds me of the interesting origin of *bába* (midwife, Hungarian). In Slavic languages (and even in Japanese), *baba* means an old woman. It may have taken on its Hungarian meaning from the fact that previously the oldest—and thus obviously the most experienced—women helped the newborn into the world. The foregoing does *not* remind me that in Spanish, "witch" is *bruja* (but *brújula* is not a little witch but a compass).

I had my own awkward interpreting experience with false cognates at a medical congress. The scientists were discussing how to kill bacteria. The English, French, and German words—*survival, survie, Überleben*—reflect the Hungarian *túlélés* (lit. over-living). I translated it verbatim into Russian: переживание [perezhivaniye]. Unfortunately for me, this term doesn't mean "survival" but "a deep experience." In fact, a Soviet delegate came up to me at the end of the session and slapped me on the shoulder: I gave evidence of a genuine humanistic approach, he said, when I dealt in such length and detail with the spiritual life of bacteria.

I am angry with the terminology for stamps, whose invention allowed simple written communication across borders. One could hope that this important means of international relations has identical or at least similar words in all languages. However, it isn't true: stamp is *bélyeg* in Hungarian, *Briefmarke* in German, *timbre-poste* in French, *sello* in Spanish, and *francobollo* in Italian.

Why don't we try to standardize international terms? There are major initiatives to this end, principally in the framework of the ISO (International Organization for Standardization). I note the draft standard DIS 1982 concerning dentistry terms. This document puts the following jungle in order:

English		**French**
Equipment	=	Matériel
Material	=	Produit
Product	=	Fourniture
Furniture	=	Mobilier

To be fair, Hungarian treats borrowed words arbitrarily as well. The original meaning of the French word *garde-robe* is, according to our classic Eckhardt dictionary,

(1) a big wardrobe;
(2) a set of clothes;
(3) the personnel of the royal wardrobe;

(4) a room lavatory;

(5) a restroom...

For the meaning in Hungarian (cloakroom, i.e., walk-in clothes closet), French uses *vestiaire*. The word *szmoking* in Hungarian doesn't mean the act of smoking; rather, it is a men's suit for formal occasions. Americans call it a tuxedo (or dinner jacket or black tie).

The original meaning of the Hungarian word *pedáns* is not meticulous but pedant, one who shows excessive learning. The Latin verb *salutare* (to greet) became *szalutálni* (to salute), and the Latin noun *virtus* (virtue) became *virtus* (bravado) in Hungarian.

One meaning of the French word *parole* is word, as in to keep one's word; it gave birth in Hungarian to the verb *parolázni* (shake hands).

I recommend to the ladies who need to start speaking Spanish: No matter how much stress they feel learning it, they shouldn't say they are *embarazada*. It means pregnant. (*Embarrassée* [French] means being embarrassed.)

A compatriot of mine excused himself from an English social gathering by saying, "My fiancée is expecting." Which, alas, means something different from her expecting him home, as he believed. With some surprise his British hosts congratulated him on the upcoming intimate family event.

It must have been even more of a surprise for the French businessman who correctly observed that a woman was expecting. His Hungarian partner said, *Monsieur, vous êtes un voyeur!* Languages are whimsical—*voyeur* doesn't mean an observant person but a sexual onlooker. I hope this gentleman was only startled and not offended.

I forgave my Russian pen pal who studied Hungarian.

Somehow he chanced upon one of my books and told me in a kind message how much he admired and loved me. He has since been closing his letters with "Your admirer and lover, Vasily."[153]

One cannot always rely on the similarities of sound, even among Slavic languages. Unfortunately, I discovered when translating that the Polish word *ołów* means lead (Pb) but the Russian олово [olovo] means tin (Sn). I also learned at my own expense that *listopad* is October in Croatian but November in Czech.[154]

However, I made my biggest blooper in a translation of a German text into Hungarian. On the basis of *Vorteil* (advantage) I could well believe that *Übervorteilung* (lit. over-advantaging) meant giving excessive advantages, whereas its meaning is just the opposite: cheating or rip-off.

---

153. The original: *tisztel és szeret* (lit. respect and love/like), hence *tisztelője és szeretője*, where the latter formation is mistaken the same way as in English.

154. Slavic languages, ostensibly similar in vocabulary, abound in false friends. An extensive collection is available in Wikibooks under "False Friends of the Slavist."

32

~

UNFORTUNATELY, because of many similar cases, "false-friend-phobia" developed in us interpreters, just as someone cheated on will see infidelity even where he or she has no reason to do so. We are afraid that the same sound is a trap, and we use a circumlocution instead. We have another phobia as well:

The excessive fear of commonplaces

Imre Éri-Halász[155] made a handy collection of "don't you say it" expressions. But this useful list sowed the seeds of anxiety in us. Our consulting editors watch like hawks for authors who smuggle a commonplace into the text.

Contrary to a poet, who is born, not made, a commonplace is made. When Sándor Petőfi first wrote that "Love is a dark pit," the metaphor was fresh and novel. It can still be novel if used in a new way, for instance to refer to a young, beautiful woman clinging to the arm of an old, tottering gallant.

A commonplace is normally a dead end. How do you respond to, "That's the way it goes"?[156] However, in our social lives there are two dead ends even more detrimental: JOKE and STORY.

A conversation begins and has almost developed into what it is meant to be: an exchange of views. But suddenly a JOKE springs to someone's mind, one out of the bountiful harvest that city folk seem to possess. The jokester tells it, and we have a good laugh.

---

155. Hungarian writer, journalist (1900–1945).
156. In the original: *Van az úgy néha.* "Sometimes it is/goes like that."

Unfortunately, however, a joke begets more. The deluge begins, and thought is engulfed.

The other cemetery of thinking is a STORY, which everybody has a stock of, most well-worn from repeated tellings. We listen to others' stories with only cursory attention, hoping it will soon be our turn to share the special story we have hiding up our sleeve.

33

~

MAY THIS CHAPTER inspire someone more competent than I to write an entire book. Let the title of this chapter be

Linguae Hungaricae Laus—
In Praise of the Hungarian Language

"How sweet your language is for singing!" the linguist Miklós Révai exclaimed in 1790.

"Let Hungarian be taught for its—perhaps true, perhaps amazing—beauty and its miraculous appeal to live on!" the professors of the Pápa Reformed College wrote to Franz Joseph I.

The war of independence failed, but the Hungarian language remained victorious.

I would like this book to remember those who didn't speak Hungarian natively but who helped it survive even at the cost of their lives. Out of the 13 Martyrs of Arad,[157] some spoke better German than Hungarian. The general Leiningen-Westerburg from Hesse, Germany, couldn't even say military commands in Hungarian. A bell was consecrated to celebrate the victory of the March revolution of 1848. Its inscription announced, "This bell was created by the confluence of faith and liberty"—in German.

A nation doesn't live only in its language

Hungarian, predicted by Johann Gottfried Herder in 1791 to

---

157. Hungarian and German rebel generals executed by the Austrian Empire after the Hungarian Revolution (1848–1849).

disappear completely, spreads our fame to the world on the wings of literary works that are barely less known than Puskás's goals.[158]

Are our Hungarian-language preservationists justified in fearing the introduction of foreign words? Has Hungarian not already eloquently proved its viability?

There is a heated debate going on about this issue in the columns of our journals and dailies. But is it a debate? No, what we see is a universal remonstrance against the air-polluting effect of foreign words. Contrary opinions arise only in the form of arguments interrupting the chorus of total rejection.

The zeal of our language preservationists is prepossessing; their cause is just. Yet sometimes I am averse to their methods. It is easy to ridicule sentences deliberately crammed with foreign words: "We negate the possibility that resistance may accumulate..."[159] But we, the more elderly, remember those who strung select flowers onto the pearly bouquet.[160] Several "deep-folk" expressions were invented and converted into sentences by Szálasi's[161] Arrow Cross Party valiants. Some "fruit" of their language cultivation movement are *disgrace-Hungarian*. Szálasi was the one who—although born in the rural fallow primeval mold—did not join the Europe-necessary reality-fixing. (From his speech delivered on June 15, 1943.) Unfortunately, they didn't publish an explanatory

---

158. Ferenc Puskás (1927–2006) was a Hungarian soccer player and manager, widely regarded as one of the greatest players of all time.

159. In the original: "*Negáljuk annak a posszibilitását, hogy akkumulálódhatik a rezisztencia.*" Instead, it could be expressed as: "*Tagadjuk annak a lehetőségét, hogy felhalmozódhat az ellenállás.*"

160. *Gyöngyösbokréta* (pearly bouquet) was the name of a folk dance revival movement between 1931 and 1944.

161. Ferenc Szálasi, leader of the fascist Arrow Cross Party–Hungarist Movement, established in 1935, then Head of State and Prime Minister between October 1944 and March 1945.

dictionary, so some notions—such as the earthness of the Earth globe or the technology management allocated to a large territory—remained somewhat vague for me.

I can still understand that the Hungaria Unified Lands have no reason to be afraid of the Plutocrat—Liberal—Freemason—Jewish—Marxist—Puritan (sic!) Anglo-Saxon leaders, since neither the English, nor the Jewish, nor the Russian peoples have soil-rooted and homeland-capable peasantry.[162] A few sentences, however, belong to the realm of psychopathology. I cite word for word:

"It is peasantry that invents writing and makes it to serve its goals, in order that in the course of long millennia its invention—the letters—would corrupt it and, through it, all the nations." (Speech in the House of Loyalty, December 5, 1942.)

Or: "The Party of National Will created its state-sovereignty foundation in its emblem with the initials of the words of popular sovereignty, which transforms the runic letters for HIT ["faith"] into the cross of the Ancient Land." (*The Goal and Demands*, Royal Hungarian University Press, 1935.)

This "true-folk" style was meant to save "deep Hungarians" from the "land parasitism" of internationalism.

---

162. Ideological terms created by the fascist Arrow Cross Party.

34

~

HOWEVER, since we are fans of our mother tongue, the overzealousness of the 1950s left a bad taste in our mouths. Some people's reaction to certain foreign words was a hallmark of their "democratism," which was cheaper than loden coats and berets.[163]

Decades have passed since the liberation. The gates of education are wide open; anyone wishing to take the chance may walk in. Sometimes I sense the indiscriminate, peevish dislike of foreign words as vestiges of the '50s: a cheap intellectual beret.

Moreover, what is a Hungarian word and what is a foreign one? If we reject foreign on principle, then we should not use *persze* (of course), which is a slavish borrowing from the Latin *per se* (by itself). We should forbid *pláne* (especially) from Hungarian lips: *plane* is also Latin (wholly, absolutely). We should devise something to replace *palánta* (seedling), as it was Hungarianized from the verb *plantare* (to plant). *Kujon* (rogue) should be reprimanded, too, as it is from the French word *couillon* (simpleton).

Are we so distrustful of the assimilating power of our language?

We urge our compatriots to make efforts to emerge from our linguistic isolation because we know that they are intellectually able to acquire one or more foreign languages.

Why don't we trust that they will also cope with foreign words, which adorn the masterpieces of our classical authors,

---

163. Loden coats, berets, and overalls were imposed by the government because they were the clothes worn by the pre-WWII working class.

make today's language more nuanced, and serve as bridges to learning other languages?

I know. Those fighting against foreign words (purists) disagree. But we tend to weed out viable flowers of international culture: Today they have been made accessible by general education to everyone. A good instinct will accept only wholesome Hungarianized forms anyway. The contrived ones will disappear, even if they originate from a stylist, such as Kosztolányi. He wouldn't for the world have uttered *autóbusz*; he used *társasgépkocsi* (lit. communal motor car) instead. Nonetheless, the former came into general use. *Televízió* didn't become *távolbalátó* (lit. farseer), *telefon* didn't become *távbeszélő* (far-speaker), nor did *autó* (car) become *gépererejű jármű* (machine-powered vehicle).[164] We rarely use the official *személyszállító kisiparos* (lit. person-transporting tradesman) instead of *maszek taxis* (self-employed taxi driver, *maszek* itself abbreviating *magánszektor* [private sector]).

I don't know if Germans gained by retaining *Sauerstoff* and *Wasserstoff* instead of the international names *oxygen* and *hydrogen*. Didn't Hungarians profit from giving up *éleny* (oxygen, from *él*, [to] live) and *köneny* (hydrogen, from *könnyű*, light [in weight]), proposed by Jókai?[165]

We fear for our beautiful language far too much. We don't trust its flexibility, its healthy instinct, with which it amalgamates all things lasting and rejects all things superfluous. Where would we be if we had shackled its development? Additions in the course of centuries from creative imagination and rustic sobriety

---

164. The word *gépjármű* did survive in the formal style, though.
165. Mór Jókai: Hungarian novelist (1825–1904). Carbon, sulfur, iron, copper, silver, tin, gold, and lead have had their own Hungarian names since ancient times. For the other elements, the international terms prevailed.

would have been *yſa pur eſ chomuv* (surely, dust and ashes) from Hungarian's first surviving texts through its multicolored diversity today.[166] As true of overprotective parents in general, our many prohibitions cause more damage than benefits to our common treasure, language.

For example, we let the passive voice, once full-fledged, fall into disuse. Kossuth[167] bid farewell to Richard Guyon[168] in 1849 by saying, "…ousted from my beloved homeland, I am compelled to become stateless…"[169]

I envy Russian, German, and English for their passive verb forms. We, too, need them because often we want to emphasize only the fact of the action, rather than the identity of the agent.

Making impersonal sentences that have a generic subject is difficult. (It is one of the reasons why clumsy constructions such as "it came to a discussion" [*vitára került*] proliferate.)[170]

Smart academic and popular articles help us make up for the loss of the passive voice by rehabilitating the *-va* / *-ve* suffix. It was high time. We almost didn't dare to sing the well-known song in its original form: *zöldre van a rácsos kapu festve* (the latticed gate

---

166. Reference to the Funeral Sermon and Prayer (aka Funeral Oration), the oldest extant contiguous Hungarian text, ca. 1200, read today as *isa, por és hamu.* The first sentence in English: "My brethren, you see with your own eyes what we are. Surely we are but dust and ashes." (Translation by Alan Jenkins)
167. Lajos Kossuth: Hungarian politician and freedom fighter (1802–1894).
168. British general in the Hungarian revolutionary army (1813–1856).
169. In the original ed.: *szeretett hazámból kiszoríttatva hontalanná lenni kényszeríttettem.* The *-tat-* and *-tet-* in the third and sixth word are obsolete passivizing suffixes. Today probably reflexive verb forms or third-person plural active forms would be used instead.
170. The passive form would be *megvitattatott*, which sounds not only obsolete but also awkward in this case. It could also be rephrased into a third person active form: *megvitatták* (they discussed it) that emphasizes the people participating, rather than the act itself.

is painted green). Even when tipsy, we felt an internal command to transform the text by the linguistic instructions: *"zöldre festették a rácsos kaput."*[171] In literary translations, I anxiously wrote sentences like *Az ki van zárva!* (It's impossible!—lit. It is shut out!). I didn't know whether a stern editor would write in the margin with a red pencil, "WHO shut it out?"

There is an option for impersonality—or better, suprapersonality, which is being above people—but it is reserved for kings and university presidents: the *pluralis majestatis* (majestic plural). More democratically but not less unequivocally than the "royal we," the elegant generic subject, used in other languages, emphasizes the nature of the message being independent of person. *Man spricht Deutsch. On parle français. Se habla español.* (lit. One speaks German/French/Spanish.) Sometimes I even feel haughtiness or self-assurance in these forms, which remind me of signs travelers meet in small French towns rich in historic monuments: *Cette ville se visite à pied* (This town is to be visited on foot.)

This impressive form works especially well in advertisements. A formerly famous grain-trading company was right in its instinct to choose this slogan:

> *Közhírré tétetik: Mauthner mag vétetik!*
> (To the public now announced:
> Mauthner seeds are to be had!)

---

171. The *van* (is) + *-va* / *-ve* (the adverbial participle of a verb) construction is a way to express the result of an action (a perfective sense), but it was discouraged for more than a century, partly because it was considered similar to the German/English passive form (where an adjective-like past participle is used) and partly because it was believed that the agent should always be specified, so only active forms should be used (as in the mistakenly proposed *festették* variant above). In fact, this adverbial passive-like construction has been part of Hungarian for many centuries. However, it is limited to cases when the action has a result.

As the passive verb forms unfortunately fall into disuse, we are compensated by the unique ability of our nouns to distinguish so elegantly between acting and occurrence: *képzés* and *képződés* (formation) or *zárás* and *záródás* (closure).[172] Other languages can envy these word pairs.

I would like a book to be written with the title *In Praise of the Hungarian Language*. It would include the names of those who, arriving from elsewhere, came to know and like this language. Among them, first of all, is Aurélien Sauvageot, who sang its praises all his life. He couldn't get enough of the beauty of words such as *ránk esteledett* (night descended upon us[173]); I fall into a reverie thinking of terms like *ihatnékom van* (I feel like drinking, lit. I have [some/the] I-could-drink).

Five Hungarian words transport us to the magic realm of fairy tales, extending between dream and reality, more beautifully than any others, in any language:

Hol volt, hol nem volt... (Once upon a time there was...)[174]

---

172. The first describes an action with reference to the doer while the second speaks of a process without an external agent involved.
173. *Ráesteledik* (night descends on him/her/It) can be regarded as a single word. *Ránk* "upon us," *este* "evening," *-(l)edik* [a verb-forming suffix].
174. Because of its ambiguity, the phrase creates a sense of mystery by way of distance and vagueness in terms of place, time, and existence: "once/wherever it/there was, once/wherever it/there wasn't..."

35

~

SKIRTING AROUND BABEL'S TOWER, I tried to weave a few thoughts that occurred to me in connection with languages into a loose fabric. Maybe it was naïve to assume that others would find as much pleasure in words' eternal variety as I do. Maybe the endeavor to try to persuade my readers to seek the joy of learning languages was only selfishness. If it was so, I will put a period to the end of my little book and excuse myself with Jókai's words:

"I wrote it for myself; it gave me much delight."

Selected References

~

Bárczi, G., L. Benkő, and J. Berrár (1967) (eds). *A magyar nyelv története* [History of the Hungarian language]. Budapest: Tankönyvkiadó.

Belyayev, B. V. (1964). *The psychology of teaching foreign languages.* New York: The Macmillan Company.

De Tena, L. (1969). *"Las vocales inglesas y las laringitis peninsulares."* New York: ABC.

Ibragimbekov, F. A. (referred to in W. F. Mackey's Bibliographie internationale sur le bilinguisme) (1982). Québec: Presses Université Laval, pp. 141, 432.

Lomb, K. (1979). *Egy tolmács a világ körül* [An interpreter around the world]. Budapest: Gondolat.

Lomb, K. (2008). *Polyglot: How I learn languages.* Trans. K. DeKorne and Á. Szegi. Berkeley, CA: TESL-EJ Publications.

Lomb, K. (2013). *Harmony of Babel: Profiles of famous polyglots of Europe.* Trans. Á. Szegi. Berkeley, CA: TESL-EJ Publications.

Papp, F. (1979). *Könyv az orosz nyelvről* [A book on the Russian language]. Budapest: Gondolat.

Sokolov, A. N. (1972). *Inner speech and thought.* Trans. G. T. Onischenko. New York: Plenum.

Index

~

Made in the USA
Middletown, DE
22 December 2019